GW00504000

Mississippi Roots
of American Popular Music

CHRISTINE WILSON, CURATOR

**AN EXHIBIT
OF THE STATE HISTORICAL MUSEUM
FEBRUARY 18 - AUGUST 31, 1990**

PATTI C. BLACK, DIRECTOR

MISSISSIPPI DEPARTMENT OF ARCHIVES AND HISTORY

ELBERT R. HILLIARD, DIRECTOR

ACKNOWLEDGEMENTS

The curator of *All Shook Up* would like to thank Patti Black, State Historical Museum director, who agreed that it was time for a major exhibit on Mississippi music and went on, despite a full work schedule, to serve as the other half of the exhibit team from careful editing of the text through configuration and design of panels and the installation of the audio component of the exhibit.

The Mississippi Department of Archives and History expresses appreciation to the following individuals and institutions for the loan of artifacts for the *All Shook Up: Mississippi Roots of American Popular Music* exhibit: Archives collection, Mississippi Department of Archives and History; Jay Barkley, Jackson, Mississippi; Blues Archive, University of Mississippi; Center for Southern Folklore, Memphis, Tennessee; Country Music Foundation, Nashville, Tennessee; Delta Blues Museum, Clarksdale, Mississippi; William Ferris, Oxford, Mississippi; Graceland, Memphis, Tennessee; Jazz Record Mart, Chicago, Illinois; William Lum, Port Gibson, Mississippi; Mississippi State Historical Museum, Jackson, Mississippi; Lillian McMurry, Jackson, Mississippi; New Stage Theatre, Jackson, Mississippi; J.C. Penney, Ridgeland, Mississippi; Piney Woods Country Life School; Smith Robertson Museum, Jackson, Mississippi; Greg "Fingers" Taylor, Jackson, Mississippi; Davis Tillman, Memphis,Tennessee; Margaret White, Jackson, Mississippi; Sam Wilkins, Jackson, Mississippi; and Wright Music Company, Jackson, Mississippi.

Special Thanks goes to the following individuals and institutions for providing information for this exhibit and catalog: Blues Archive of the University of Mississippi, the Country Music Foundation, Andy Anderson, Stanley Booth, Dave Clark, Teddy Edwards, William Ferris, Alvin Fielder, Carl Fleischhauer, Ray Funk, Lillian McMurry, Charlie Musselwhite, Jim O'Neal, John Reese, John Sumrall, Woody Sistrunk, Gayle Wardlow, Freddie Waits, Dick Waterman, Tim Whitsett, Charles Wolfe.

The Phil Hardin Foundation of Meridian provided partial support for the publication of *All Shook Up: Mississippi Roots of American Popular Music*. The Foundation joins the Mississippi Department of Archives and History to support this and other projects that make our state's cultural heritage accessible to Mississippians in and out of the classroom.

ISBN 0-938896-65-2
Library of Congress Number 95-620650
Copyright © 1995 Mississippi Department of Archives and History

Robin Smith, designer

Cover photograph courtesy Center for Southern Folklore, Ernest Withers, photographer

TABLE OF CONTENTS

Introduction

INTRODUCTION

THE EARLIEST AND FINEST BLUES MUSICIANS CAME OUT OF MISSISSIPPI. Eric Clapton summed that up when he called Muddy Waters "my father." And most people know that Elvis, called by some the greatest single influence on popular culture in the twentieth century, was born and bred in Mississippi.

What is not generally recognized is the phenomenal influence of Mississippi artists in other genres of popular music: Jimmie Rodgers of Meridian originated what we now call "country music"; Sam Cooke of Clarksdale, a sensual gospel singer, set the standard for crooners ever since; and Lester Young of Woodville improvised his way out of swing, leading generations of jazz artists with him. All of these artists didn't emerge out of a vacuum, of course, and the exhibit *All Shook Up: Mississippi Roots of American Popular Music* was designed to suggest the breadth and richness of this state's musical environment, an environment created through a mixing of the music of two cultures, a combining of all the elements that make up that experience we call music.

Why did it happen here? Black and white people were living and working in close proximity in a poor state where music was the central leisure activity for both. Blacks lived around large plantations that served as networks for musicians travelling among them, sharing and borrowing music until different "schools" of music were created over the state. And even though formally separated by a social system, blacks and whites could not deny the meeting place provided by music.

A stimulating physical environment – storms, floods, hurricanes, extreme heat and drought, bringing destruction, change, renewal – served as a catalyst to the imagination and passion felt by blacks and whites enduring those forces together. The abundantly green, fertile, and wild landscape was full of names evocative of Indian cultures. A heritage of the Old Southwest and its larger-than-life heroes set the stage for more of the same and created a place where an ordinary working man like John Henry or a blues singer like Robert Johnson could become, in a matter of decades, a folk hero for all time.

And there was the River, a beacon even for those who had never seen it, a symbol of hope and adventure, escape to something better, an open highway that they knew was always there, if all else failed – and hope fuels art.

Music that emerged from Mississippi has shaped the development of popular music of the country and the world. Major innovators created new music in every form – gospel, blues, country, R&B, rock, and jazz. Mississippi's music was the product of the mixing of two traditions – black and white – with scales, rhythms, idioms, techniques, tonalities, and repertories intermingling for over a century to produce new music that was so rich and compelling it inspired strong new directions for the development of American popular music.

Christine Wilson, Curator
All Shook Up: Mississippi Roots of American Popular Music

INTRODUCTION

THE EARLIEST AND FINEST BLUES MUSICIANS CAME OUT OF MISSISSIPPI. Eric Clapton summed that up when he called Muddy Waters "my father." And most people know that Elvis, called by some the greatest single influence on popular culture in the twentieth century, was born and bred in Mississippi.

What is not generally recognized is the phenomenal influence of Mississippi artists in other genres of popular music: Jimmie Rodgers of Meridian originated what we now call "country music"; Sam Cooke of Clarksdale, a sensual gospel singer, set the standard for crooners ever since; and Lester Young of Woodville improvised his way out of swing, leading generations of jazz artists with him. All of these artists didn't emerge out of a vacuum, of course, and the exhibit *All Shook Up: Mississippi Roots of American Popular Music* was designed to suggest the breadth and richness of this state's musical environment, an environment created through a mixing of the music of two cultures, a combining of all the elements that make up that experience we call music.

Why did it happen here? Black and white people were living and working in close proximity in a poor state where music was the central leisure activity for both. Blacks lived around large plantations that served as networks for musicians travelling among them, sharing and borrowing music until different "schools" of music were created over the state. And even though formally separated by a social system, blacks and whites could not deny the meeting place provided by music.

A stimulating physical environment – storms, floods, hurricanes, extreme heat and drought, bringing destruction, change, renewal – served as a catalyst to the imagination and passion felt by blacks and whites enduring those forces together. The abundantly green, fertile, and wild landscape was full of names evocative of Indian cultures. A heritage of the Old Southwest and its larger-than-life heroes set the stage for more of the same and created a place where an ordinary working man like John Henry or a blues singer like Robert Johnson could become, in a matter of decades, a folk hero for all time.

And there was the River, a beacon even for those who had never seen it, a symbol of hope and adventure, escape to something better, an open highway that they knew was always there, if all else failed – and hope fuels art.

Music that emerged from Mississippi has shaped the development of popular music of the country and the world. Major innovators created new music in every form – gospel, blues, country, R&B, rock, and jazz. Mississippi's music was the product of the mixing of two traditions – black and white – with scales, rhythms, idioms, techniques, tonalities, and repertories intermingling for over a century to produce new music that was so rich and compelling it inspired strong new directions for the development of American popular music.

Christine Wilson, Curator
All Shook Up: Mississippi Roots of American Popular Music

BLUES

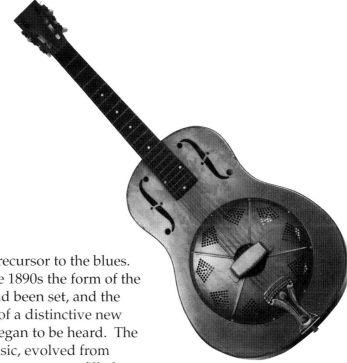

THE BLUES WERE BORN IN THE MISSISSIPPI DELTA, the product of a lengthy and hard labor. The blues were songs of hope, born out of work and out of sorrow: from rhythmic work chants of railroad gangs and cotton pickers; from spirituals; from "sorrow" slave songs; and from the haunting and lyrical field hollers. During the Civil War, black soldiers improvised spiritual-like chants about daily marching and other toils of war. In the chants they shifted to a half-dissonant middle part, forming a song that was a direct precursor to the blues.

By the 1890s the form of the blues had been set, and the sounds of a distinctive new music began to be heard. The new music, evolved from African sources, was filled with the polyrhythms and tonalities of African music and bore the nuances of many different tribes. But the new black Americans had also borrowed substantially from white man's music – its musical scale, most importantly, and patterns from its rich folk music traditions. The blues

"Mississippi, especially Mississippi blues, in all its forms, is the single most important root source of modern popular music."

Jim O'Neal, music historian

Founding editor, *Living Blues*

magazine

1

"My mother was married to a sanctified preacher. And while the adults were having dinner first, before the children, he would put his guitar on the bed. As soon as they would close the kitchen door, right on the bed I would go! So finally one day he caught me. But he didn't do what I thought he was gonna do. Instead of bawlin' me out, he taught me three chords. And I still play those three chords...There was a group then called the Golden Gate Quartette—somethin' like the Staple Singers are today. And that is they sing spiritual songs and usually with a beat and with a feelin'. So that's what I wanted to do."

B. B. King

"Blues is a steal from spirituals."

Big Bill Broonzy

had not emerged from Africa; it was born out of two musical cultures – black and white – that were thriving and growing separately and together. Blacks took white music and adapted it, bent its parts, literally, to create a style that could express both the despair and the hope of their lives.

The result of this large-scale mixing of two separate cultures was a sound that became the basis of mainstream popular music for the entire 20th century. From musical gatherings on plantations like Dockery's came rhythms, lyrics, bass patterns, even gui-

tar riffs that were to spread over the world, coursing through a broad spectrum of styles, from pop to jazz to country, classical, rock and beyond.

Although blues had roots in religious music, blues and church music—and, later, gospel music—were strictly separated. Blues singers, almost always starting out in the church, eventually had to make a choice—sometimes a painful one—between the two conflicting but similar genres and their corresponding ways of life.

"My mother started me singin' spirituals when I was about four years old with her in church...We started a little group when I was about ten or eleven — a little quartette — and we would use the guitar to tune us up. But we couldn't go into the Baptist Church because of the guitar."

B. B. King

"When you hear people singing hymns in church—these long, drawn-out songs—that's the blues. Yeah. Church music and the blues is all one and the same. They came out of the same soul, same heart, same body."

Johnny Shines

"The onliest difference between the cotton pickin' blues and what we doing today is tempo. We using practically the same words."

Frank Frost

WHAT IS THE BLUES?

A classic blues song is made up of twelve bars, in an AAB structure: The first four-bar line establishes a situation: "When a woman gets the blues, she wrings her hands and cries." Repeated with addition of a pickup word or phrase: "I said, when a woman gets the blues she wrings her hands and cries." The final answering line is different: "But when a man gets the blues, he grabs a train and rides." Here is a sample notation:

HIGH WATER EVERYWHERE- Charley Patton

The use of drums was forbidden to slaves, but the need for the African beat was still strong. The blues answered that need, with a beat so implicit that the drum was not needed. The form that evolved to accommodate that beat was a simple one, made up of twelve bars, but one that provided room for endless improvisation, another tradition of African music. It was this quality of improvisation that, along with the blue notes, or diminished notes, was to provide the soul of another American genre, jazz.

"I used to say to Son House, 'Would you play so and so?' cause I was trying to get that touch on that thing he did. Bukka White got a thing I been trying to learn for five years, and I ain't learnt it yet."

Muddy Waters

Juke Joints

With the growth of the blues came the spread of the phenomenon known as the "juke joint." In these makeshift buildings that served as social clubs, the blues developed and bloomed. Songs and lyrics were borrowed, adapted from musicians who travelled from joint to joint; techniques and styles were copied and elaborated upon; young bluesmen found mentors and left home to follow them in a life on the road.

"Joe Williams came to Greenwood in 1932 when I was about seventeen. He played a country dance one Saturday night, oh, about a half a mile from my house, across the fields...So I left with Joe Williams, started playing around. We traveled to Vicksburg, Natchez, New Orleans, down the Gulf Coast—riding buses and hitch-hiking, with guitars on our shoulders—just going."

Honeyboy Edwards

"I made just as much as the guy who worked five days, .75 a day. I used to make $2.50 on Saturday night at a frolic, or supper, with my guitar, and you couldn't make but $3.75 for five days' work."

Muddy Waters

"We had these little juke joints, little taverns at that time...On the week-end like Saturday night you might stay out all night cause there was usually some little place in the alley we would call that stayed open all night—that was all right with the people down-town and they would allow them to stay open. We called them Saturday night fish fries, you know, they had two or three names they called 'em— juke houses and suppers."

Muddy Waters

"The biggest thing around Curley's Barrelhouse (in Vicksburg) at that time would be piano players. You could hear Little Brother Montgomery's tunes there and 'Black Snake Blues.' Charley Patton came from Vicksburg and a whole bunch of piano players used to come around there."

Willie Dixon

"They played Stellas. They played old cheap Stella guitars–across the board."

Gayle Dean Wardlow, music historian

Sam Chatmon

The Guitar

The guitar came to be the instrument of the blues. Throughout the 19th century the most common instrument among both blacks and whites had been the fiddle. W. C. Handy, in his *Blues: An Anthology,* tells that his original band, organized in the first decade of this century, consisted of a cornetist (Handy), a guitarist, a bass player, and three fiddlers.

Blues guitarists developed in the midst of the fiddle tradition: fathers of many well known bluesmen were fiddlers, and bluesmen often incorporated fiddle music into their songs. Following the Civil War and the industrial revolution in the North, mass production of guitars began. The steel-string guitar appeared, providing more volume and solid tone than the earlier gut strings. The guitar proved to be an almost ideal instrument for the blues. It provided the heavy back beat that fulfilled the African taste for drum rhythm. It was available and cheap, with some models going for $2.50 from the Sears and Roebuck catalog. It was light and mobile, good for travelling, and it was expressive, capable of a range of effects as various as the musicians who played it.

Another inexpensive instrument, the harmonica, became a stock resource of musicians travelling from joint to joint. It could express and imitate the nuances of the human voice, and would fit in a back pocket easily. Harmonica-playing skills were, like those for the guitar, taught and handed down from musician to musician. For example, Mississippi's Howlin' Wolf was one of the many bluesmen who learned "harp" from premier harpist Sonny Boy Williamson.

> ### BLUE NOTES
>
> *The blues gets its name from "blue notes," which some musicologists say originated in Africa. The third, fifth, and seventh notes are flatted to produce chords that come together only in quarter tones. Stringed instruments, like the guitar, can "bend" notes in this way, producing the dissonant sound of the blues.*

"Blue notes" were effectively produced on the guitar, and techniques were developed to make the solo guitar sounds even more expressive. Some of the techniques were holdovers from the one-strand or ditty-bow—like the bottleneck style of playing. W. C. Handy mentions 1892-1903 as the years when he first heard, in Tutwiler, "the weirdest music I ever heard." He listened to a black man playing his guitar strings with the blade of a knife, "bottleneck" style.

W.C. Handy

"In the twenties to the forties, records were a household item. People had handwound phonographs; they were available on the installment plan from McMurry's Furniture Store in Jackson. Records were 10¢. People would get off from work on Saturday, go down and buy a record."

Ben Bailey, music historian

"White folks didn't buy enough records to put in your eye. Basically it was a black market. We bought a few hillbilly and pop records, but basically it was a black market."

Lillian McMurry,

Diamond Record Co.

Radio/Recording

The blues was spread regionally through itinerant musicians, but the mixing of influences and styles was made dramatic with the introduction of blues records and radio shows. In 1922, rural musicians began to be recorded, and soon record companies realized there was a good-sized market for these records.

Though they borrowed heavily from records, blues musicians interpreted the material in their own styles, creating new music.

Sonny Boy Williamson (Rice Miller) (center) recording the King Biscuit Hour, broadcast from Helena, Arkansas, and heard over the Delta via WROX radio.

Performers borrowed both music and lyrics from records. Some musicians used the term "records" when referring to a blues tune whether it had been recorded or not.

"You have to get verses out of records. You can get a verse out of each record and make you a recording of your own."
James Son Thomas

H.C. Speir

H.C. Speir ran a music store in Jackson and as a local talent scout for blues, recorded over 200 sides, featuring artists such as Charley Patton, Son House, Skip James, the Mississippi Sheiks, Robert Johnson, Tommy Johnson, and almost every other blues singer working during the 1930s in Mississippi. His influence on American music was so great that it has been compared to that of Sam Phillips at Sun Studios and the Chess Brothers at Chess Records.

"First Speir found Charley Patton at Dockery's Plantation. He got out and looked for talent...He scouted all the time...If it hadn't been for Speir, Mississippi's greatest natural resource might have gone untapped."
Gayle Dean Wardlow, music historian

QUESTION: *How did you get hold of Robert Johnson's records?*
MUDDY WATERS: *"In the little town I was around they didn't have just a definite record store, you know, they had, like, they'd sell everything like, uh, shotgun shells and pistols, everything, including records. My aunt, her name was Jemima, she used to buy a lot of records and she had records of Blind Lemon Jefferson and people like that. Well, as a growing boy, it seemed like those records seemed to sink in my head."*

Lillian McMurry

As founder of Diamond Record Company in Jackson (publisher of Trumpet and other labels) Lillian McMurry recorded Sonny Boy Williamson, Elmore James, Willie Love, and others. She also managed the Record Mart, one of the largest record shops and mail order businesses in the region. She bought radio time for the store, and the "Record Mart Show" beamed out to six states.

In the 1940s, independent record companies began to bloom across the country, offering the work of Mississippi artists to receptive listeners. Savoy, Aristocrat, and Atlantic were early labels that recorded Mississippi musicians.

Willie Love

Sonny Boy Williamson

Elmore James

Charley Patton

Charley Patton was the first of the Mississippi bluesmen to emerge from the anonymous folk tradition. Born near Edwards around 1885, he moved to Dockery Plantation to work and played around the Delta at jukes, dances, fish fries, and house parties from 1897 to 1934. Patton travelled with Son House, tutored Howlin' Wolf, and inspired countless others. He recorded for Paramount, 1929-30, and Vocalion, 1934. He died in Indianola in 1934.

"He recorded all those records for all them people, RCA Victor. When he died, just had a marker on his grave...Stuck on here was his name, Charley Patton, had a little paper over it, you know."

Honeyboy Edwards, musician

"Patton inspired just about every bluesman of consequence. He is among the most important musicians 20th-century America has produced."

Robert Palmer, music historian

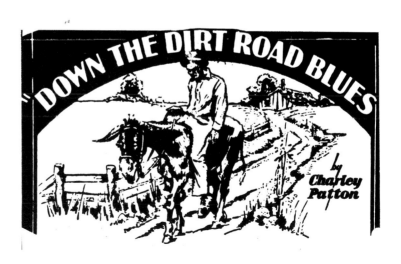

"You know, I hear other guys talk about when Robert learned to play the guitar, but I don't think he ever learned. He was doing it when they thought he was learning. They don't talk about a duck learning to swim, do they?"

Johnny Shines, musician

Columbia Records' two-CD complete Robert Johnson recordings has been an international best-seller, already far beyond its platinum record, the highest sales award.

"I can figure out almost anybody's licks – but not his."

Keith Richards, Rolling Stones

Robert Johnson

Robert L. Johnson, the most potent legend in all the blues, was born near Hazlehurst in 1912 and ran away from home as a teenager to learn guitar from Son House. He worked the Delta with his music, then travelled through the upper South and East. He played with Son House, Sonny Boy Williamson, Howlin' Wolf, Elmore James, and Honeyboy Edwards. His recording sessions in 1936-37 produced some of the richest music in the history of the blues: "Crossroads," "Love in Vain," "Hellhound on my Trail," and "Dust My Broom," among others. His guitar and vocal

"His [Robert Johnson's] music has become the root source for a whole generation of blues and rock and roll musicians."

Samuel B. Chartres,
music historian

skills established a foundation on which generations of blues and rock musicians have been building ever since. Robert Johnson was poisoned in 1938 while playing at a juke joint in Greenwood at the age of 24.

A one-ton monument memorializing Robert Johnson stands in Mt. Zion Missionary Baptist Church Cemetery, Morgan City, Mississippi.

Tommy Johnson

Tommy Johnson

Born in Crystal Springs in 1896, Tommy Johnson ran away from home to play in jukes and medicine shows, and he played the Delta from 1912 until 1935. He played with Charley Patton, Ishmon Bracey, K. C. Douglas, and others and recorded for Victor and Paramount. In 1935 he moved to Jackson and performed in central Mississippi until his death in 1956 in Crystal Springs.

Son House

Eddie "Son" House was born in Coahoma County in 1902. Often regarded as the quintessential blues singer, he did not begin performing until his mid-20s. He was first a preacher, an influence that shaped his forceful style. In 1930 he recorded for Paramount "Preachin' the Blues" and an account of the farming crisis in the Mississippi Delta, "Dry Spell Blues." Son House is especially known for his affecting vocal style and his bottleneck slide technique. Son House was rediscovered in the 60s and for a decade played to blues festivals and college audiences.

Son House

"For thirty years, Tommy Johnson was the most important and influential blues singer in the state of Mississippi."

David Evans, blues scholar

"Tommy Johnson was a pretty heavy drinker and he'd get high sometimes. But he was a good musician. I liked to hear him sing that song about 'I asked her for water and she gave me gasoline.'"

Rev. Lacy, musician

"He is remembered as the epitome of the Delta blues."

New Grove Gospel, Blues and Jazz

Skip James

Bukka White

Skip James

Nehemiah "Skip" James from Bentonia influenced countless bluesmen with his plaintive, high-pitched voice, rapid guitar technique, and poetic lyrics. One of his best-known and most representative songs is "I'm So Glad."

Mississippi John Hurt

Born in Teoc, John Hurt lived in Avalon working as a farmer and railroad laborer but never played professionally. His songster's repertory preserves old traditions and includes "Frankie," "Stack O' Lee Blues," and "Spike Driver Blues."

Bukka White

Booker T. Washington White, born in Houston, Mississippi, recorded on many labels and played 60s blues festivals, including the Newport Folk Festival. His best-known songs include "Aberdeen, Mississippi, Blues," and "When Can I Change My Clothes."

Mississippi John Hurt

ALLSTARS

Woodrow Wilson Adams/*Tchula*
Garfield Akers
Mose Allison/*Tippo*
Ada Mae Anderson
John Arnold
James Baker
Sam Baker/*Jackson*
Dick Bankston
Will Batts/*Benton County*
Nathan Beauregard/*Ashland*
Arthur Bell,
Carey Bell/*Macon*
Iverson Bey/*Vicksburg*
Johnnie Billington/*Clarksdale*
Ernest Blair/*Coldwater*
Lucille Bogan/*Amory*
Charlie Booker/*Sunflower County*
Eddie Boyd
"Little" Joe Blue /*Vicksburg*
Ishmon Bracey/*Hinds County*
Jan Bradley/*Byhalia*
"Blind" James Brewer /
Brookhaven
Jessie Mae Brooks
Dusty Brown/*Tralake*
Andrew Brown/*Jackson*
Elijah Brown/*Macon*
John Henry
"Bubba"Brown/*Rankin County*
Melvin Brown
Robert Brown/*Itta Bena*
Willie Brown/*Drew*
"Little" George Buford/*Hernando*
Ranie Burnette
Eddie Burns/*Belzoni*
James "Butch" Cage /*Hamburg*
Joe Callicot/*Nesbit*
Lucie Campbell/*Duck Hill*

Jack Owens

Gus Cannon/*Red Banks*
Ace Cannon/*Grenada*
Sam Carr
Jeanne Carroll/*Ruleville*
Bo Carter/*Hinds County*
Leonard Caston/*Sumrall*
Walter Chapman
Armenter "Bo" Chatmon/*Bolton*
Peter "Memphis Slim"
Chatmon/*Bolton*
Sam Chatmon/*Hollandale*
Boyd Childney
Eddie Clearwater/*Macon*
Willie Cobbs/*Greenwood*
Louis "Bo" Collins/*Indianola*
"Bogus" Ben Covington/*Lowndes
County*
Arthur "Big Boy" Crudup/*Forest*
James "Peck" Curtis/*Bolivar
County*
Eddie Cusic
"Big" Ike Darby/*Neshoba County*
Maxwell Street Davis
Walter Davis/*Grenada*
"Blind" John Henry

Davis/*Hattiesburg*
Paul Davis/*Greenville*
James "Jimmy" Dawkins/*Tchula*
Mamie Davis
Bonnie Delaney/*Pontotoc County*
William "Do-Boy"
Diamond/*Canton*
Robert Diggs/*Friars Point*
Willie Dixon/*Vicksburg*
K. C. Douglas/*Madison County*
"Memphis" Minnie
Douglas/*Walls*
Scott Dunbar/*Wilkinson County*
Hezekiah Early and the House
Rockers/*Vicksburg*
David Edwards/*Shaw*
"Honeyboy" Edwards/*Shaw*
Billy "the Kid" Emerson
Frank Floyd/*Toccopola*
Cora Fluker/*Marion*
Willie Foster/*Greenville*
"Little" Willy Foster
Leroy Foster/*Pontotoc County*
Eugene Fox

*Houston Stackhouse, Sonny Boy
Williamson, Peck Curtis*

Theodore Frye/*Fayette*
Johnny Fuller/*Edwards*
William "Jazz" Gillum/*Indianola*
Boyd Gilmore/*Humphreys County*
Bobby Grant
Danny Green
Lee Green
Lillian Green
Shirley Griffith/*Brandon*
Homer Harris/*Drew*
William Harris
Provine Hatch/*Sledge*
Ted Hawkins/*Lakeshore*
Sid Hemphill
John Lee Henley/*Lawrence County*
Raymond Hill
Rosa Lee Hill/*Como*
Tony Hollins
Joe Holmes/*McComb*
Myrt Holmes
Morris Holt/*Grenada*
Roosevelt Holts/*Walthall County*
Walter Lee "Big Daddy"
Hood/*Bentonia*
Earl Zebedee Hooker
John Lee Hooker/*Clarksdale*
Son House/*Riverton*
Luther Henry Huff/*Rankin County*
"Mississippi" John Hurt/*Avalon*
Bo Weevil Jackson
Lee Jackson/*Jackson*
"Little" Walter Jacobs
Elmore James/*Richland*
Skip "Nehemiah" James/*Bentonia*
"Big" Jack Johnson
Luther "Guitar" Johnson/*Itta Bena*
Mary Johnson/*Eden Station*
Oliver "Dink" Johnson/*Biloxi*
Robert L. Johnson/*Hazlehurst*

Charlie Musselwhite

Cleveland "Broom-Man" Jones

Tommy Johnson/*Crystal Springs*
Wallace Johnson/*Pine Top*
Willie Lee Johnson/*Tate County*
Compton Jones
Elmore Jones/*Canton*
Henry Jones/*Vicksburg*
Johnny Jones/*Jackson*
O. D. Jones
Kenneth Kidd/*Newton County*
Rev. Rubin Lacey/*Rankin County*
Furry Lewis/*Red Banks*
Alexander "George" Lightfoot
Harry Lipson
John Lomax/*Durant*

Clayton Love/*Clarksdale*
Willie Love/*Duncan*
Albert "Sunnyland Slim"
Luandrew/*Vance*
Aubrey Lyles/*Jackson*
Lee "Lee Mack"
MacMillan/*Brookhaven*
John Wesley Macon/*Lowndes County*
Sam Maghett/*Grenada*
Thomas T. Marshall
Jake Martin/*Mound Bayou*
"Fiddlin" Joe Martin/*Hinds County*

Tommy McClennan/*Yazoo City*
Charlie McCoy/*Jackson*
James McCoy/*Drew*
Big Joe McCoy/*Hinds County*
"Mississippi" Fred
McDowell/*Batesville*
Hayes B. McMullen/*Tutwiler*
Elsie McWilliams/*Meridian*
Rick McWilliams/*Meridian*
Louis Meyers/*Byhalia*
Rice "Sonny Boy Williamson II"
Miller/*Glendora*
Jake Moore/*Oak Grove*
Johnnie B. Moore/*Clarksdale*
Sam Myers/*Laurel*
Isaiah Nettles
Alvin "Youngblood"
Nichols/*Camden*
Hammie Nixon
Dale Norris/*Springfield*
William James "Deadeye"
Norris/*Jackson*
Sam "One Leg" Norwood/*Crystal
Springs*
Jack Owen/*Bentonia*
Eli Owens
Junior Parker/*Clarksdale*
Charley Patton/*Edwards*
Joe Willie "Pinetop"
Perkins/*Belzoni*
Jimmy Phillips/*Greenville*
Eugene Powell/*Greenville*
James Edward "Snooky"
Pryor/*Lambert*
Herb Quinn
Eddie Raspberry/*Jackson*
Mathis James Reed/*Dunleith*
Fenton Robinson/*Minter City*
Jesse Robinson/*Jackson*
Gail Robinson/*Meridian*
Jimmie Rodgers/*Meridian*
Charles Isaiah "Doc" Ross/*Tunica*

Son Thomas

Marie Selika/*Natchez*
John Sellars
J. D. Short/*Claiborne County*
"Little" Hudson Shower/*Sharkey
County*
John B. Sillers/*Clarksdale*
Henry "Son" Sims
Tommy Smiley
Albert Smith/*Bolivar County*
Leo Smith/*Leland*
Moses Smith/*Jefferson County*
Willie Mae Ford Smith/*Rolling
Fork*

Otis Smothers/*Lexington*
Willie Spann/*Hinds County*
"Big Boy" Spires/*Bentonia*
Bud Spires/*Yazoo City*
Houston Stackhouse/*Wesson*
Staples Singers (Roebuck "Pop"
Staples)/*Drew*
Jewell "Babe" Stovall/*Walthall
County*
Henry Stuckey/*Bentonia*
Napoleon Strickland/*Como*
James Douglas Suggs/*Attala*

Fred McDowell,
Arthur Crudup,
Robert Pete Williams

Thompson/*Centreville*
Dione Thomas/*Lambert*
Henry Townsend/*Shelby*
James Monroe Trotter/*Grand Gulf*
Othar Turner/*Gravel Springs*
C. V. Veal
Monroe Vincent/*Woodland*
Mose Vinson/*Holly Springs*
Walker Jacob "Vincent"
Vinson/*Bolton*
John "Big Moose"
Walker/*Washington County*
Wade Walton/*Lombardy*
Louis "Kid Thomas"
Watts/*Oktibbeha County*
Esau Weary
"Boogie" Bill Webb/*Jackson*
Booker T. Washington "Bukka"
White/*Houston*
PeeWee Whittaker/*Natchez*
Nelson "Dirty Red"
Wilborn/*Tallahatchie County*
Joe Willie Wilkins/*Davenport*
Rev. Robert Timothy
Wilkins/*Hernando*
"Big" Joe Williams/*Crawford*
Joseph "JoJo" Williams/*Coahoma*
Lee "Shot" Williams/*Holmes*
County
Gerald Stanley Wilson/*Shelby*
Willie Wilson/*Drew*
Matilda Witherspoon/*Hattiesburg*
Big John Wrencher
Johnny Young/*Vicksburg*
Isaac Youngblood

County
Sweet Miss Coffy/*Jackson*
Tommy Tate/*Jackson*
Theodore R. "Hound Dog"
Taylor/*Natchez*
Eddie "Playboy" Taylor/*Bolivar*
County
H.D. Taylor/*Natchez*
Johnny "Geechee"
Temple/*Canton*
"Doc" Terry/*Sunflower County*
James "Son" Thomas/*Leland*
Willie B. Thomas/*Bolivar County*
Alphonso "Sonny"

COUNTRY

COUNTRY MUSIC, IN
MISSISSIPPI AS IN
OTHER SOUTHERN
STATES, began with fiddle
tunes and folk ballads from
England, Ireland, and
Scotland. During the 19th century, Mississippi musicians felt
the influence of popular music,
through travelling tent and
medicine shows and minstrel
shows like the Rabbit Foot
Minstrels from Vicksburg.
After the large national touring shows broke up, the music
survived in regional vaudeville shows.

John Anderson Brown, Iuka

HAMILTON. L. M.   Leach.

Mountains of Is - rael,   rear on high   Your sum-mits crown'd with verdure new; And spread your branches to the sky,   Re-fulgent with ce-les-tial dew.

Sacred Music

"Sacred Music" was a huge influence on country music, just as black sacred music had in part spawned the blues. The church was most southerners' earliest opportunity for singing, and the Great Revival, beginning about 1801, intensified the role of hymn-singing in southern life. "Singing conventions" became common; participants would sing songs combining hymns, folk elements, and popular music. Songbooks were printed, using a method of notation called shape-note, in which pitch was indicated by means of differently shaped notes: diamond, square, triangle, etc. The shape-note method and its resulting style (also called Sacred Harp singing) had originated in New England, where it was used to help semi-literate congregations cope with music on a printed page. Use of the shape-note method died out in New England, but it survived in the South, where people considered it as much a cultural tradition as a practical device. The sounds of shape-note singing, with its distinctive minor harmonies, went on to influence gospel, rhythm and blues, and even rock and roll.

Blackwood Brothers

White gospel music changed at the end of the l9th century when professional harmony quartets began to tour the South. Since the audience for country music was much the same as that for gospel, the influence was strongly felt. Mississippi groups like Ward Hurd and the Bibletones, the Singing Churchmen, and the Central Mississippi Quartette were popular. The Blackwood Brothers Quartet was formed in 1934 in Ackerman by three brothers: Roy, Doyle, and James, all sons of a Delta sharecropper and his wife.

The fourth member was the young son of Roy, R. W. The group began broadcasting on radio in Jackson in 1937, singing gospel, pop, and country tunes. The Quartet became one of the most influential singing groups in the nation, defining the quartet style that became the backbone of classic southern gospel music.

Claunch Family

String Bands

String bands, recalling English country fiddling in such songs as "Sallie Gooden" and others, were formed by blacks and whites alike. They persisted into the 20th century through minstrel shows, vaudeville, and house parties. Made up of fiddle, banjo, and guitar, the string band gradually shifted into the domain of white country musicians. The rural string tradition—reflecting both black and white influences— was strong in the South and, along with vocal harmonizing, became one of the bases of what was later called "country music." Mississippi bands that recorded on national labels included Mumford Bean, the Leake County Revelers, and the Mississippi Sheiks.

Mississippi Sheiks

The Mississippi Sheiks were an influential black string band made up of brothers Armenter ("Bo") and Sam Chatmon and for a time, their half-brother, bluesman Charley Patton. The group, which featured much fiddling, also incorporated blues, and the resulting mixture was to influence both black and white country and blues bands. The Sheiks toured the South, playing country dances, picnics, and fish fries. The Sheiks recorded on the OKEH label.

Every member of the Chatmon family of Bolton played at least one instrument and performed regularly in the area.

Chatmon Family

John Hatcher, Iuka, 1939

An Unexampled Sale of Violin Outfits,

The human voice is probably the most important element in country music, but the fiddle, banjo, and guitar became the traditional country instruments. These instruments moved back and forth between the black and white traditions with musicians exchanging riffs and other techniques, until the rural string band genre began to be called "country music."

Mississippi's earliest settlers brought fiddles with them from Europe and the British Isles. Fiddlers who played traditional tunes were in demand in Mississippi for all types of social occasions – weddings, dances, log raisings – and distinct fiddling styles developed in different areas of the state. It was the fiddle that gave country music tunes the minor-key quality that is still prevalent in the genre.

The style of Mississippi fiddler W. T. Narmour was the prototype for modern bluegrass and blues-influenced fiddling.

The guitar, brought to the New World by early settlers, became the mainstay of cowboys, Yankee and Confederate soldiers, and, later, black blues singers and string bands in the South.

The banjo has been called the only native American instrument, but its ancestry can be traced to an African instrument, the *banza.* Throughout the first half of the 19th century the banjo was associated exclusively with black musicians. Gradually, through minstrel shows primarily, the banjo transferred to the white folk tradition.

Ernest Claunch

The Kitrells

*At WJDX microphone, Jackson:
Slim Scoggins and the Roamin'
Cowboys*

During the 1920s a number of national record companies began to record the music of Mississippi string bands. Ralph Peer, who also scouted for blues musicians, came to Tupelo in 1928 and auditioned. Hoyt Ming and his Pep Steppers became the first of several Lee County string groups to record for RCA Victor.

A striking feature of these records is the "hollering," or chiming in with high notes at the end of phrases. The notion of an Indian whooping or hollering inside a fiddle tune was an old one and probably in the same tradition as Jimmie Rodgers' "blue yodel."

In 1928 the OKEH record company arranged to record the music of George Carter of Monroe County. The sessions were recorded in Memphis. When the company wanted to take George, his brother Andrew, and son Jimmie to England to record, they declined. According to Jimmie Carter, "The man says, 'We want him to go with us over across the water...'My daddy was willing but my uncle said, 'No that's too far away from home.' "

Hoyt Ming and The Pep Steppers

Leake County Revelers

The Leake County Revelers, the most famous string band to come out of Mississippi in the 1920s, grew popular through their Columbia records, appearances on tour, and their regular Saturday evening programs on WJDX, broadcasting out of the Lamar Life Building in Jackson. The true home of the Revelers was not Leake County but Sebastopol in Scott County. Members were R.O. Mosely, mandolin; Jim Wolverton and Will Gilmer, banjo; and Dallas Jones, guitar.

Music for recording was often obtained by local talent scouts, usually the local record store owner. In Winona, the record store owner was A. M. "Doc" Bailey. Bailey signed for RCA Victor, among others, the Mississippi Possum Hunters of Winona (Lonnie Ellis, John Holloway, and Pete Herring); Narmour and Smith of Carroll County; and the Ray Brothers of Choctaw County. Bailey also arranged for Vocalion label recordings by Carroll County fiddler Gene Clardy, with guitarist Stan Clements, and the Attala County band led by fiddlers Luke Milner and Luke Curtis.

Radio

While string bands and other old-time country music were being heard on stations like WSB in Atlanta, few Mississippi stations were established or strong enough to have regular audiences. Aside from "independent"—non-FCC registered—record store stations, the earliest station in the state was WCOC in Meridian, which opened in 1927, the same year as the Grand Ole Opry in Nashville, which played country music on WSM for fans in the hills of north Mississippi.

Radio station WJDX, established in Jackson in 1930, was the second in Mississippi after WCOC in Meridian.

Jimmie Rodgers

Jimmie Rodgers, born near Meridian, became the single most influential singer in country music history. Born September 8, 1897, Jimmie Rodgers was working with his father's railroad crews by age 14 and learned the language and music of railroadmen. In his off hours he occasionally played guitar and banjo with black musicians down around Tenth Street in Meridian. In 1925 he signed on as a black-face entertainer with a touring medicine show. With a string band he formed the Jimmie Rodgers Entertainers and began making stage appearances and singing on radio station WWNC.

In 1927, he recorded the first of his twelve blue yodels, which became the hillbilly hit of the year.

"All contemporary country singing is clearly attributable to Rodgers' compositions, themes, and styles."
John Greenway, music scholar

"The most inspiring type of entertainer for me has always been somebody like Jimmie Rodgers, somebody who could do it alone and was totally original. He was combining elements of blues and hillbilly sounds before anyone else had thought of it...he wasn't just another white boy singing black. That was his great genius and he was there first."
Bob Dylan, musician

"Legend has it that in his heyday, general store customers would approach the counter and say: 'Let me have a pound of butter, a dozen eggs, and the latest Jimmie Rodgers record.'"

Bill Malone, country music scholar

The structure of his songs was typically blues, but at the end of the third line, Rodgers would lift his voice an octave—the blue yodel that made him famous.

Elsie McWilliams, the sister of Rodgers' wife Carrie, played piano in an early trio with Jimmie Rodgers and wrote music for him. Her compositions were tailor-made for Rodgers, emphasizing his strengths, which she knew well. Although most of Rodgers' recordings carry his name as composer, he actually wrote very litle, depending on Elsie McWilliams for about a third of his material, with the rest coming from Tin Pan Alley and other sources.

Between 1927 and 1933, Jimmie Rodgers became the first country music star to attract a national audience. He died at the height of his career in 1933, from tuberculosis.

"The music I chose, personally, to listen to, was country music. I don't know why it was exactly. People are always saying to me, 'Why don't you sing this way or that?' You know, as a matter of my pigmentation. Like whether you were pink or purple or whatever really should determine in some kind of absolute way the kind of music you like. That's kind of silly, isn't it? I mean it's all American music, anyway."

Charley Pride

Charley Pride

A Sledge native, Charley Pride made his first RCA recordings in 1965. Pride's singing had such a pure country sound that no one suspected he was black until they saw his pictures on albums. Pride has had over 40 gold and platinum records.

Frank Floyd

Born in Toccapola in 1908, Frank Floyd played medicine shows with his hillbilly-talking blues style. He was a favorite on many radio shows through the years and had his own show in the early fifties. Floyd was a self-proclaimed spokesman for poor farmers, sharecroppers, rounders, hobos, and others of the poor rural South. He recorded on Chess and Sun labels, among others.

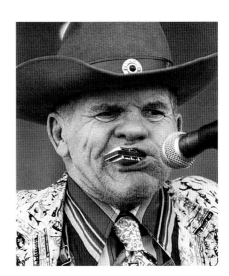

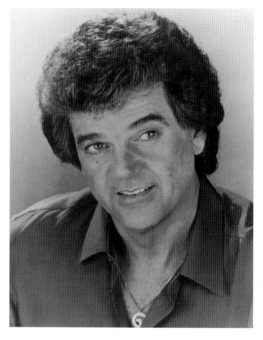

Tammy Wynette

Born Virginia Wynette Pugh in Itawamba County, Tammy Wynette has recorded numerous albums and had two number one songs: "Stand By Your Man" and "My Elusive Dreams."

Conway Twitty

Born at Friars Point, Harold Lloyd Jenkins picked his stage name from Conway, Arkansas, and Twitty, Texas. The son of a riverboat pilot, he learned to play a guitar by the age of six and by ten had his own band. At twelve, he was appearing regularly on the Helena, Arkansas, radio station. Twitty, whose biggest hit was "It's Only Make Believe" in 1958, holds the record for the most number one singles of all contemporary country musicians.

O.B. McClinton

Senatobia native O. B. McClinton wrote, produced, and performed hits on such labels as Epic, STAX, and CBS Records.

ALLSTARS

Carvel Lee "Mississippi Slim" Ausborn
Martha Baldwin/*Florence*
Moe Bandy/*Meridian*
Mumford Bean and his Itawambians/*Itawamba County*
Howard Barron
Bibletones
Blackwood Brothers/*Ackerman*
Eddie Bond
Rod Brasfield/*Smithville*
Bill Bruner
Jimmy Buffet/*Pascagoula*
Paul Burlison/*Jackson*
Carter Brothers and Sons/*Monroe County*
Johnny Carver/*Jackson*
Central Mississippi Quartet
Chapman Family/*Centreville*
Gene Clardy/*Carroll County*
Claunch Family
Stan Clements/*Carroll County*
Hank Cochran/*Greenville*
Collier Trio/*Carthage*
Mike Compton/*Meridian*
Emmett Connor
Van Cook/*Purvis*
Stan Crawford/*Natchez*
Luke Curtis/*Attala County*
Paul Davis/*Meridian*
Duck Hillbillies
Buddy Durham/*Hattiesburg*
Kathy Edge/*Booneville*
Stoney Edwards
Farmer Sisters
Charlie Feathers/*Myrtle*
Frank Floyd/*Toccapola*
Carlton Freeny/*Carthage*
Freeny's Barn Dance

Blackwood Brothers (later generation)

Band/*Carthage*
Bobbie Gentry/*Greenwood*
Carlton Gilmer/*Walnut Grove*
Morgan Gilmer/*Walnut Grove*
Graves Brothers/*Hattiesburg*
Mark Gray/*Utica*
Rev. C. M. Grayson/*Magee*
Jason Guthrie
Angela Hall /*Laurel*
Boots Harris/*Jackson*
Henderson Brothers
Faith Hill/*Jackson*
Kim Hill /*Starkville*
Al Hopson
Hopson Brothers
Carl Jackson/*Louisville*
Harold Lloyd "Conway Twitty" Jenkins/*Friars Point*

Canoy Wildcats

Faith Hill

Dallas Jones/*Sebastopol*
J. L. Jones and the Good
Guys/*Pearl*
Kim Kays/*Laurel*
Kay Kellum/*Jackson*
Murray Kellum/*Jackson*
Stan Kesler
Kim Keys/*Laurel*
Carl Knight/*Jackson*
Fred Knoblock/*Jackson*
Jodi Labelle/*Lumberton*
Leake County Revelers/*Sebastapol*
Jerry Lee Lewis/*Ferriday, Natchez*
Warner Mack/*Vicksburg*
Madden Community
Band/*Madden*
Alvis Massengale/*Newton County*
Meridian Hustlers/*Meridian*
Dion Jackson/*Natchez*
O. B. McClinton/*Senatobia*
Bob McCree/*Jackson*
Luke McDaniel/*Jackson*

Scott McQuaig
Elsie McWilliams/*Meridian*
Rick McWilliams/*Meridian*
Luke Milner/*Attala County*
Floyd Ming/*Ackerman*
Hoyt Ming and his
Pepsteppers/*Tupelo*
Mississippi Possum
Hunters/*Winona*
Michael Pyron and the Dry
County Blues Band/*Duck Hill*
Mississippi Sacred Harp Singers
Mississippi Sheiks/*Bolton*
Billy Mitchell/*Tupelo*
Narmour and Smith/*Carroll
County*
Nations Brothers/*Winchester*
Newton County
Hillbillies/*Newton County*
James O'Gwynn
Paul Overstreet/*Vancleave*
Justin Peters/*Jackson*

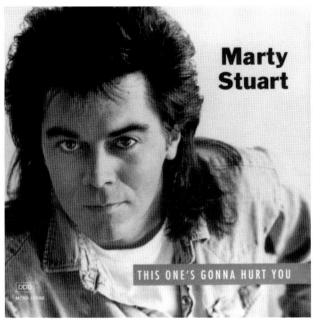

Marty Stuart

Jimmy Phillips/*Greenville*
"Red" Pleasant/*Tupelo*
Elvis Presley/*Tupelo*
Bob Price/*Tishomingo County*
Charley Pride/*Sledge*
Virginia Wynette "Tammy Wynette"
Pugh/*Itawamba County*
Ray Brothers/*Choctaw County*
Ovan Ray
Billy Ray Reynolds/*Sullivans Hollow*
Bobby Roberts
Jimmie Rodgers/*Meridian*
Grady Russell/*Leake City*
Grover Russell/*Leake City*
Johnny Russell/*Moorhead*
Ford Rush
Judy Ryals
George Sandifer/*Jackson*
Slim Scoggins and the Roamin'
Cowboys/*Clinton*
E. L. "Mutt" Scoggins/*Clinton*
Johnny Sea/*Gulfport*

Jim Weatherly

35

Jimmy Swan

Bobby Gentry

Frank Self/*Greenville*
Gene Simmons/*Tupelo*
Singing Churchmen
Singing Ryals Family/*Walthall County*
Ben Shae/*Grenada County*
Howard Smith
The Steeles/*Magee*
Doug Stevens/*Lee County*
Marty Stuart/*Philadelphia*
Jimmy Swan/*Jackson*
Merle "Red" Taylor
Marguerite Tew/*Laurel*
Hayden Thompson
Derrick Townsend/*Laurel*
Herman Truelove/*Starkville*
Jimmy Weatherly/*Pontotoc*
Ernest Wilson
Tony Williams/*Laurel*
Jim Wolverton/*Sebastopol*
Johnny Work

Paul Overstreet

GOSPEL

BLACK GOSPEL MUSIC IS ROOTED IN SPIRITUALS, l9th-century hymns, shape-note songs, blues, and ragtime.

Spirituals were popularized by the Jubilee Singers from Fisk University, who toured the nation and were imitated by other large choirs throughout the l9th century.

Fisk Jubilee Singers

"The 'swing' of spirituals is an altogether subtle and elusive thing, because it's in perfect union with the religious ecstasy that manifests itself in the swaying bodies of a congregation. It is very difficult if not impossible to sing these songs sitting or standing still and at the same time capture the spontaneous 'swing' which is of their very essence."

James Weldon Jones, Preface,

Book of American Negro Spirituals

Utica Jubilee Quartet

Spirituals

The first musical notation of spirituals, published in 1867, captured little of their character—their rhythmic complexities, "blue" notes, glissandos, growls, and call-and-response patterns.

Large spiritual-singing choirs began to be replaced in the 20th century by smaller harmonizing groups, usually called quartets. Competition between groups promoted harmonizing skills, and quartets began to tour the nation and Europe on entertainment circuits.

The Utica Jubilee Quartet made a successful three-month European tour in the late 1920s. The group, made up of students from Utica Institute, was probably the first black quartet to be regularly featured in a national radio program in America.

Hymns brought in during the Great Awakening, a religious movement of the 1730s, had spread among both black and white churches, and the new, livelier tunes of composers like Isaac Watts began to replace scriptural texts and spirituals.

Like rural white churchgoers, blacks used shape-note hymnals, collections like *The Sacred Harp.* Often black communities had their own *Colored Sacred Harp* – used in addition to or instead of the white collection. Blacks also developed a parallel tradition, seven-shape-note singing.

> *"The true roots of black gospel and spirituals can be traced to the extraordinary collision of cultures that took place at the beginning of the 18th century, as African slave met English church hymn."*
> **Viv Broughton, music scholar**

Cotton Blossom Singers

Changing trends in popular religious music were evident in groups active at the Piney Woods Country Life School near Braxton. Principal Laurence Jones organized the Cotton Blossom Singers in 1922, as a fund-raising quartet.

Within the decade, thirteen groups such as this one were touring the country. They stopped travelling when gasoline was rationed during World War II, but they continued to sing on radio broadcasts on twenty-one stations.

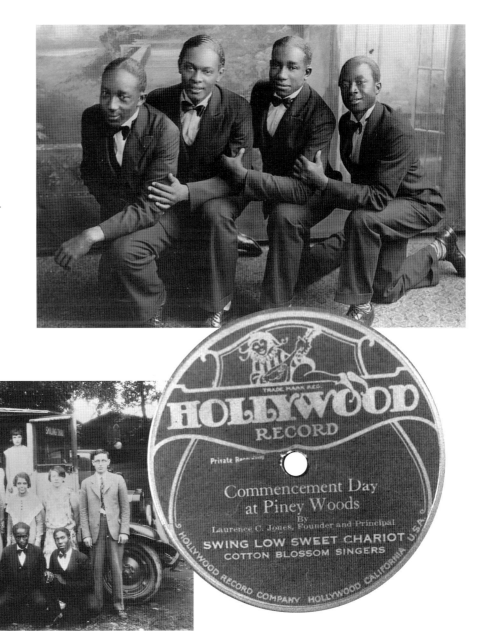

Five Blind Boys

The Five Blind Boys of Mississippi were also formed at Piney Woods School in 1943. Originally called the Jackson Harmoneers, the Five Blind Boys were indeed all blind. They left school in 1944, travelling all over the South playing in packed auditoriums. Many of their early recordings were unaccompanied vocal harmonizing; others have piano and drum that provide rhythm. The Five Blind Boys were among those chosen in 1965 to tour Europe in the first "Spiritual and Gospel Festival, presenting the very best of America's black gospel."

PEACOCK RECORDING   JACKSON HARMONEERS   Exclusive Management HERALD ATTRACTIONS

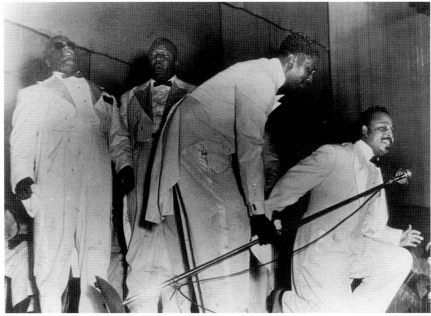

"They had a formidable reputation as a live gospel act. So much so that for a while in New Orleans they were required by the mayor to put up a peace bond because they were sending so many members of the congregation to the hospital."

Arthur Brownlee, member, Five Blind Boys

Staples Singers

Of the gospel groups influenced by the blues, the one most directly linked was the Staples Singers, led by Roebuck Staples (born in Winona, 1914), who worked on the same plantation as blues singer Charley Patton. The blues was an influence on his guitar playing, but he was also attracted to the music of his father's Methodist church. Roebuck "Pop" Staples is said to have introduced the guitar into the Methodist Church, where gospel music was slow to be accepted, and was the first major gospel singer to use the electric guitar. He formed the Staples Singers with his son Purvis and daughters Cleotha, Mavis, and Yvonne in Chicago, Illinois, 1948.

"There's something about the gospel blues, that's so deep the world can't stand it."

Sister Rosetta Tharpe, gospel singer

"I grew up in the Delta—in Drew. They're all from the Delta—Big Bill [Broonzy], Son House, all of them. That's what inspired me, listening to all that blues down there."

Roebuck ("Pop") Staples

Musical Preaching

Preaching styles and gospel music developed together, with improvisation, rhythm, and special vocal techniques common to both. Emphatic words were injected in a syncopated rhythm in the musical parts of the church service just as they were during sermons – "Yes, Lord," "Hallelujah," and "Help Me, Jesus" – and became part of gospel music.

Charles Price Jones

Charles Price Jones (1865-1949) of Jackson founded the Church of Christ Holiness denomination. A musician himself, he wrote and published hymns for his church choir.

C. H. Mason

In 1895 C. H. Mason founded the Church of God in Christ in Lexington, Mississippi. The sect developed rapidly, and with the migrations north in the 20th century, the denomination became established in Chicago, Detroit, and other cities. By 1945, they made up four-fifths of the 500 black churches in Chicago. The Church of God in Christ became a crucial base for the development of gospel music.

C.H. Mason

Charles Price Jones

C. L. Franklin

Clarence LaVaughn Franklin, born near Indianola in 1915, gained fame for his preaching in Clarksdale, Greenville, and Memphis before he became pastor of the 4,500-member New Bethel Baptist Church in Detroit. He went on to record more than seventy albums of his preaching and singing that sold widely over two decades and strongly influenced the work of many musicians, including his daughter Aretha. Known as the "jitterbug preacher," Franklin went around the country on preaching tours and in 1963 led the Freedom March in Detroit that attracted over two hundred thousand people, setting a prototype for Martin Luther King's march in Washington later that summer.

C.L. Franklin and daughter Aretha, right.

Soul Stirrers

"The Soul Stirrers were the beginning of a more emotional style that represented a change from both the rhythmic spirituals and the previous quartets."

Ray Funk, music historian

"It makes no difference what kind of song you sing. You have to stir up the emotion of the 'congregation' and literally lift them from their chairs. I learned this lesson at an early age in church."

Sam Cooke

The Modern Quartet

The style of the modern quartet was established by a group called the Soul Stirrers, led by Mississippian Sam Cooke. The Soul Stirrers, organized in 1945, were the first to add a fifth man to the quartet, thus providing four-part harmony for the lead singer; the first to use guitar accompaniment; the first to give concerts consisting solely of gospel music; and the first religious group to have a weekly radio show of their own, in 1940.

The Soul Stirrers also influenced physical presentation in singing. Quartets before the Soul Stirrers sang standing still and straight. The Soul Stirrers introduced movement that punctuated the emotional quality of the gospel message. Sam Cooke carried his own gospel style and that of his predecessor R. H. Harris into rhythm and blues and rock and roll, influencing groups like the Platters and almost all later crooners.

Willard and Lillian McMurry

"All the big stars used to make personal appearances at the Record Mart promoting their local bookings. Then we'd load up and go on up to the radio station and do interviews on the Record Mart Show. I remember Joe Liggins, The Trumpeteers, Charles Brown, Lowell Fulson and Ray Charles on the same show."

Lillian McMurry

Southern Sons

Gospel on Record

By 1940, small recording companies were beginning to release records by harmonizing groups, most of them called "quartets." After World War II, gospel music got its own national radio show, "Gospel Train," in New York, and by 1945, gospel singers were becoming recording stars and influencing the development of rhythm and blues, rock, and jazz.

The Diamond Record Company was founded in 1950 by Lillian McMurry of Jackson to issue gospel records. Diamond's label ,"Trumpet,"

named after Gabriel's trumpet in the Bible, featured spirituals and gospel music by well-known national gospel groups like the Southern Sons Quartette, the St. Andrews Gospelaires, and others.

"Groups of black men would crowd into the booths and I found out they were singing spirituals along with the records. Some of them were really good, too! I started thinking, 'Why can't I make a record?' Gads, I didn't know what I was getting into."

Lillian McMurry, Trumpet Records

In the 20th century, gospel music retained its deeply emotional quality but became more sophisticated as it developed in the urban environment. Recordings show the evolution: first there was the gospel choir, with piano and small percussion; then in the 50s, electric organ, amplified guitars, and drums were added; during the 70s, strings, bass, and added percussions made gospel music fully orchestrated.

In Hattiesburg, Blind Roosevelt Graves and his half-blind brother Uaroy Graves had an exhilarating small band, the Mississippi Jook Band; they played ragtime and blues, but recorded principally gospel songs. The crossover influences are evident.

Cleophus Robinson

The Reverend Cleophus Robinson, internationally known preacher and gospel singer, has been presented at Washington's Constitution Hall, Carnegie Hall, the Apollo Theatre, and Lincoln Center for the Performing Arts. He recorded over 200 albums and had a weekly television show in fifteen major American cities.

Frank Williams

A Smithdale native, Frank Williams was lead singer and major songwriter in the widely popular gospel groups the Jackson Southernairs and the Williams Brothers. While managing production of all gospel records at Malaco Records in Jackson, he formed the award-winning Mississippi Mass Choir in 1988 and served as its principal singer. Using the best of two mediums in gospel music, the choir and the quartet, Williams pioneered a new gospel sound that he called "choirtet."

The Christianaires

ALLSTARS

Willie Banks and the Messengers/ *Jackson*
Richard Bryant
Campbell College Quartet/ *Jackson*
Canton Spirituals/ *Canton*
Chambers Brothers/ *Flora*
Chapman Family/ *Centreville*
Fannie Bell Chapman/ *Centreville*
Christianaires/ *Sontag*
Cotton Blossom Singers/ *Piney Woods*
Elder Curry
Delta Big Four
Five Blind Boys/ *Piney Woods*
Four Stars
C. L. Franklin/ *Clarksdale*
Theodore Frye/ *Fayette*
Glorybound
Glory Mountain Singers

Gold Star/ *Hattiesburg*
Roosevelt Graves/ *Hattiesburg*
Graves Brothers/ *Hattiesburg*
Son House/ *Riverton*
Jimmy Jones
Kelly Brothers
Riley "B.B." King/ *Indianola*
Brother Joe May/ *Macon*
Meditation Singers
Mississippi Mass Choir/ *Jackson*
Mississippi Sacred Harp Singers
Dorothy Moore/ *Jackson*
Reverend Mosely
Charley Patton/ *Edwards*
Pilgrim Jubilees
Mary Pinckney
Cleophus Robinson/ *Canton*
Rust College Quartet/ *Holly Springs*
Boyd Rivers
Ernestine Rundles
Teresa Scott/ *Jackson*
Seven Stars

Utica Quartet

The Seven Stars

Seven Star Juniors
Willie Mae Ford Smith/*Rolling Fork*
Smith Brothers/*Jackson*
Soul Stirrers (Sam Cooke)/*Clarksdale*
Southern Sons/*Winona*
Southernaires/*Jackson*
Spiritual Clouds of Joy/*Jackson*
Staples Singers (Roebuck Staples)/*Winona*
Union Jubilee
Utica Jubilee Quartet/*Utica*
Voices of Hope/*Natchez*
Williams Brothers/*Smithdale*
Elder Roma Wilson/*Hickory Flat*
Early Wright/*Clarksdale*
Yazoo and Mississippi Valley Group

Willie Banks and the Messengers

Eddie and the Corinthians

The Canton Spirituals

Williams Brothers

Mississippi Mass Choir

URBAN BLUES

EARLY IN THE 20TH
CENTURY SOUTHERN
BLACKS BEGAN to
migrate to northern cities
where jobs and civil rights
held promise of a better life.
When country blues performers reached the city, they were
exposed to tin pan alley and
other musical traditions and to
a new urban environment. By
the end of the 1930s a synthesis
of styles was emerging: the
Chicago blues. As one musi-
cologist put it, "The blues
came out of Mississippi,
sniffed around in Memphis,
and then settled in Chicago."
After World War II, a new
wave of Mississippi musicians
arrived in Chicago, where the
blues recording industry had
discovered increasing audiences for urban blues.

Big Joe Williams

To overcome the din of club crowds, guitars and harmonicas were amplified and drums were added, forming the "blues band," which was to be a major influence on rock and roll. The guitar—solo instrument of the blues—remained the centerpiece of the blues band, with its hard-driving rhythms and "bottle-neck" sound, now electrified.

One of the first Mississippians to take the blues to Chicago was Big Bill Broonzy of Scott, who arrived there in 1920. He began playing "for chicken and chitlin at Saturday night rent parties." By the late 1930s Broonzy was one of the most popular performers in the country. He became a mentor to many later influential Mississippi bluesmen in Chicago.

Chicago was the home of the race records industry: Paramount, Bluebird, and Vocalion were based there, and early Chicago bluesmen like Broonzy recorded on these labels.

Big Bill Broonzy

Howlin' Wolf at Silvio's, Chicago

"*I was playing a lot of Elmo James stuff, it was on Fifty-ninth and State, right on the el there, sell barbecue on one side and chicken on the other side. And Magic Sam, he was right opposite the el on the west side of the street, and I went in there and we played.*"

Honeyboy Edwards

But it was with Leonard and Phil Chess and the founding of Chess/Checker Records that Chicago blues established an identity, a distinctive and urgent "Chicago Blues" sound that superseded the former "smooth" city blues style of Broonzy and others.

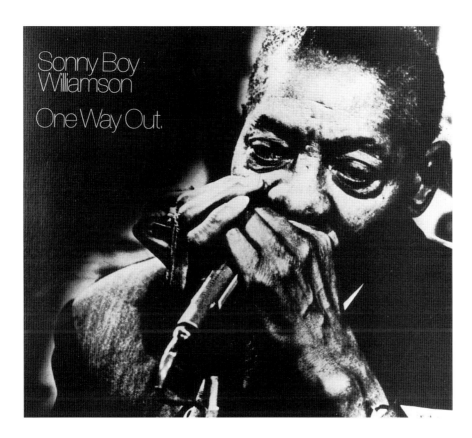

Charlie Musselwhite

Big Walter Horton

James Cotton

The Blues Harp

Sonny Boy Williamson (Rice Miller) of Glendora was the star of KFFA's "King Biscuit Time" radio show and had already recorded on Jackson's Trumpet label before moving to Chicago and to Chess Records. Williamson, along with Big Walter Horton of Horn Lake, developed electrified harmonica styles that were to influence all harp players after them, including Tunica's James Cotton and Kosciusko harpist Charlie Musselwhite, a white man who broke racial barriers to play nightly with black Southside Chicago blues musicians.

Muddy Waters

Muddy Waters, who was born in Rolling Fork in 1915, became the "King of the Chicago Blues" and set a new style for blues musicians. First recorded by the Library of Congress at Stovall Plantation in 1941, McKinley Morganfield had learned from Charley Patton and Son House, but he had also learned from records. In 1943 the uncle for whom Muddy worked as a truck driver gave him an electric guitar. Soon afterwards Big Bill Broonzy presented Muddy Waters at Sylvio's, a Southside club in Chicago. In 1947 he began to make his name on Aristocrat Records (later Chess). "Hoochie-Coochie Man," 1954, sold over 75,000 copies. "Rollin' Stone," 1950, sold 80,000 copies and inspired Bob Dylan's single and the name of the British group led by Mick Jagger.

"No single bluesman has had more direct nor more personal influence on the development of rock music in America and in England than has Muddy Waters."

Bruce Cook, music historian

"I had a part of my own, part of Son House, and a little part of Robert Johnson...I never actually seen Robert play...I thought he was real great from his records."

Muddy Waters

"I think they released mines [record] on a Friday. By noon. He [Leonard Chess] pressed up 3,000 and delivered 'em and you couldn't get one in Chicago nowhere. They sold 'em out, the people buying two or three at a time."

Muddy Waters

Howlin' Wolf

Born in West Point in 1910, Chester Burnett (Howlin' Wolf) started recording in Memphis with Sam Phillips. Wolf's strangest influence was white blues yodeler Jimmie Rodgers, the country singer from Meridian. "I couldn't do no yodelin', so I turned to growlin', then howlin' and it's done me fine," Wolf said. In 1952 he moved to Chicago, where his fierce, gravelly voice and falsetto howl earned him his name. At six feet tall and 250 pounds, Wolf often crawled onstage on all fours, baring his teeth and growling. Wolf's 1950-51 Phillips recordings were purchased by Chess Records in Chicago, where his career flourished. Two of his most popular hits were "Evil Going On" and "Spoonful."

> *"I was raised on blues and spirituals; but after you wake up to a lot of facts about life, you know, the spiritual thing starts to look kind of phony in places. So this is one of the reasons I took off to the blues."*
>
> **Willie Dixon**

Willie Dixon

Born in Vicksburg in 1915, Willie Dixon sang in a quartet before moving to Chicago in 1926. By the 1940s he was playing string bass with his own band. A multi-talented musician, he wrote over 200 hits for Chess Records, including "Hoochie-Coochie Man," "Wang Dang Doodle," and "Little Red Rooster." The source of most of the songs recorded during the urban blues era, Dixon is considered the "granddaddy" of the Chicago blues.

Over fifty rock acts have recorded his songs, including Elvis Presley, Chuck Berry, Van Morrison, Eric Clapton, and the Allman Brothers.

Dixon wrote, for Muddy Waters, "I Just Want to Make Love to You," "I'm Ready," and others; for Howlin' Wolf, he wrote "Evil," "Spoonful," "Back Door Man," "Built for Comfort," "Little Red Rooster," and "Three Hundred Pounds of Joy," among others. For Little Walter, he wrote "My Babe"; and "Mellow Down Easy"; for Otis Rush, tunes like "Can't Quit You Baby" and "Pretty Thing"; and for Bo Diddley, "You Can't Judge a Book by Looking at Its Cover."

B. B. King

As the Chicago blues audience began to fade, B. B. King was creating his own brand of urban blues in Memphis. King was born Riley King in Indianola in 1925. A member of the St. John Gospel Singers in his youth, he retains a heavy gospel strain in his music. He also incorporates the sounds of the jazz that he played on the air as a radio disc jockey for WDIA.

King's music is marked by clean, biting, single-note guitar solos and is played with large bands with full horn sections (saxophones, trumpets, trombones).

B.B. King, perhaps the country's most celebrated bluesman, has recorded over sixty albums and has appeared in concert all over the world, where his most requested song is "The Thrill is Gone."

"My eyes are closed. I forget what I look like. In fact, I don't even care what I look like because the feeling that I got through what I'm doin' is so important."
B. B. King

Otis Spann, right, with Muddy Waters, left

> *"There was no way to avoid it. On a spring day (in Chicago) people would be sitting out on their porches playing Charley Patton or Otis Rush. You just heard it everywhere."*
> **Elvin Bishop, musician**

Otis Rush

Otis Rush of Philadelphia moved to Chicago as a teenager, where he performed in clubs throughout the fifties and was a prime originator of the West Side blues style. He launched the Cobra record label with his hit "Can't Quit You Baby," then in the sixties recorded for Chess, Duke, and Atlantic labels, among others, and on the Vanguard anthology of Chicago blues.

Otis Spann

Born in Jackson, brilliant blues pianist Otis Spann recorded with Muddy Waters, Howlin' Wolf, Bo Diddley and many others and was house pianist for the Chess label through the 50s and into the 60s. He recorded under his own name for Chess/Checker from 1955 until 1963.

Albert King

Albert King, who was born near Indianola, developed a signature guitar style and achieved his first hits on the Stax label, backed by the Memphis soul rhythm section and horns. During the sixties he produced one of the most influential blues albums of the decade, *Born Under a Bad Sign*.

Peavey Electronics

Hartley Peavey of Meridian played guitar in numerous bands around the state as a young man and ended up building sound equipment for each one. In 1965 he founded Peavey Electronics, which offered guitars, amplification, and PA systems. By 1980 the company was a leader in the industry, distributing world-wide, with major artists in every field of music using and endorsing Peavey gear.

"I'm in this business for one reason. I love music."

Hartley Peavey

The Blues Revival and the International Connection

The blues were unknown in Europe until Big Bill Broonzy's music was introduced there in the early 1950s. In 1961 Willie Dixon and Memphis Slim organized the first American Folk Blues Festival in Paris, and for a time this annual event took Chicago blues to major cities in Europe.

Through the 1960s rock bands adapted or copied the music of Mississippi bluesmen. Today the Mississippi Delta bluesmen continue to be revered and studied much more widely in Europe than in the United States.

Pictured: Mississippians Little Brother Montgomery, Otis Rush, Big Joe Williams, and Jimmy Dawkins.

"I had to go to Berlin, Germany, to hear a song by Johnny Fuller of Mississippi."
Mose Allison

Willie Dixon at Orly Airport, Paris.

"What kind of audience did you have back then—was it all black?" Muddy Waters: "All black, all black. But now later, lately, up in the 50s whites started to coming out to see me from Chicago University. They'd take a chance to come out in the black neighborhoods to be with us."

Muddy Waters

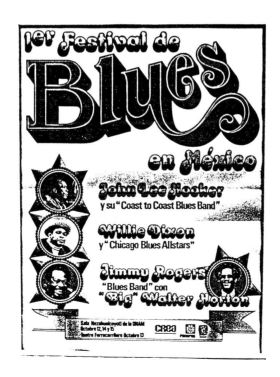

ALLSTARS

Larry Addison/*McComb*
Roosevelt "Booby" Barnes/*Longworth*
William Lee "Big Bill" Broonzy/*Scott*
Eddie Burks/*Greenwood*
Chester Arthur "Howlin' Wolf" Burnett/*West Point*
Ace Cannon/*Grenada*
Eddie "The Chief" Clearwater/*Macon*
James Cotton/*Tunica*
Arthur "Big Boy" Crudup/*Forest*
Jimmy Dawkins/*Tchula*
Willie Dixon/*Vicksburg*
"Honeyboy" Edwards/*Shaw*
Walter Lee "Big Daddy" Hood/*Bentonia*
Walter Hooker
John Lee Horton
Little Walter Horton/*Horn Lake*
Jim Jackson /*Hernando*
Elmore James/*Richland*
Luther "Guitar, Jr." Johnson/*Itta Bena*

Eddie "Guitar Slim" Jones/*Greenwood*
Albert King/*Indianola*
Riley "B. B." King/*Indianola*
Kinsey Report
"Big Daddy" Kinsey/*Pleasant Grove*
J. B. Lenoir/*Monticello*
Clayton Love/*Clarksdale*
Willie Love/*Duncan*
Albert "Sunnyland Slim" Luandrew/*Vance*
Sam "Magic Sam" Maghett/*Grenada*
Fred McDowell/*Como*
McKinley "Muddy Waters" Morganfield/*Rolling Fork*
Rice "Sonny Boy Williamson II" Miller/*Glendora*
Charlie Musselwhite/*Kosciusko*
Sam Myers/*Laurel*
Junior Parker/*Clarksdale*
Joe Willie "Pinetop" Perkins/*Belzoni*
Jimmy Reed/*Leland*
Jimmy Rogers/*Ruleville*
Otis Rush/*Philadelphia*

Irene Scruggs
Brother John Sellers/*Clarksdale*
Lucille Spann/*Jackson*
Otis Spann/*Jackson*
Houston Stackhouse/*Wesson*
Hubert Sumlin/*Greenwood*
Greg "Fingers" Taylor/*Jackson*
Theodore R. "Hound Dog" Taylor/*Natchez*
Ike Turner/*Clarksdale*

Big Daddy Hood

Pinetop Perkins

Big Jack Johnson

Eddie Clearwater

Honeyboy Edwards

RHYTHM AND BLUES

FEELIN' GOOD MUSIC

RHYTHM AND BLUES, WHICH REVITALIZED POPULAR music after World War II, developed from urban blues and the increasingly popular black gospel music. Basically blues with the addition of a heavier backbeat and rhythmic modernizations, R&B absorbed other elements directly from the church: emotionality, tempo, style. Showmanship was a big part of the R&B scene, with saxophone players swinging their instruments into the air and quartets working out dance "routines" to accompany the music.

Jackson club, c. 1950

"Race Records," a title of pride given them by the *Chicago Defender*, were available on selected subsidiary labels of larger record companies and on black-owned labels like Peacock. The music, also referred to as "race music" in the 1930s and 1940s, was given a new name—rhythm and blues—by Jerry Wexler of Atlantic Records in 1949.

Early R&B was dominated by Mississippi blues singers: Big Boy Crudup of Forest, John Lee Hooker of Clarksdale, and Guitar Slim of Greenwood.

"Big Boy" Crudup

Originally a gospel singer in a quartet, Arthur "Big Boy" Crudup moved from Forest to Chicago, where he began playing blues at street/house parties. One of the first to accompany his singing on electric guitar, Crudup made some of the first electric "race records." By the 1940s he was one of the most popular blues singers and recorded on Bluebird, Trumpet, Checker, Ace, Victor, and Delmark labels, among others. A highly respected songwriter, Crudup was sought after to appear in 70s blues revival concerts such as the Newport Jazz Festival. One of Elvis Presley's favorite Crudup songs was "That's All Right, Mama," which Presley recorded as a hit in 1954.

Big Boy Crudup

Rufus Thomas

Rufus Thomas of Cayce made a splash with his recording "Bear Cat," which answered Big Mama Thornton's "Hound Dog," later recorded by Elvis Presley. Thomas, a Rabbit Foot Minstrel in his youth, also created a dance craze of the early 60s with his "Walkin the Dog."

Guitar Slim

Guitar Slim

Guitar Slim (Eddie Jones) of Greenwood sang in local church choirs in Hollandale before heading for New Orleans where he teamed up with piano great Huey Smith. Guitar Slim recorded on various labels and toured the South and Southeast regularly during the 50s before playing the famous Apollo Theatre in New York in 1954. He died an early death in 1957 at the age of thirty-three, but is regarded as a seminal figure in the development of R&B nationally.

Little Junior Parker

Little Junior Parker of Clarksdale put "Feelin' Good" and "Love My Baby" on regional R&B charts. Parker's "Mystery Train" became an even bigger hit when covered by Elvis Presley in 1955.

Junior Parker

C.L. Franklin

C. L. Franklin, Clarksdale preacher, had a huge influence on R&B music. His daughter Aretha, the "Queen of R&B," drew heavily on the preaching style of her father and also on the musical style of gospel singer Mavis Staples of the Staples Singers, Sam Cooke, and others who frequented the Franklin home.

"Mahalia and Sam Cooke...were always in the house. Any excuse for singing the good old gospel songs was taken up and Aretha would often sit in the corner and watch as the shouting, clapping, and moaning went on all through the night."

C.L. Franklin

John Lee Hooker

Functioning as both bluesman and commercial R&B singer was John Lee Hooker of Clarksdale, whose "Crawlin' Kingsnake" and "Boogie Chillen" in 1948 and 1949 were hits on the Modern label. On the VeeJay label, Hooker pursued an even more rhythmic sound with "Boom Boom" in 1962.

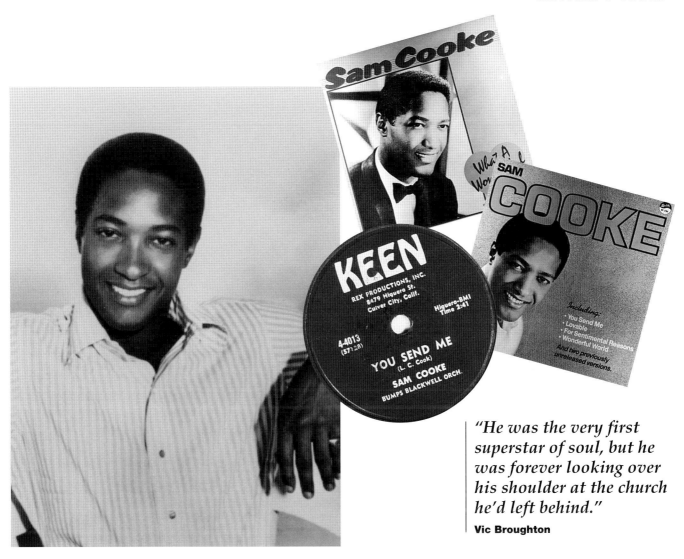

"He was the very first superstar of soul, but he was forever looking over his shoulder at the church he'd left behind."

Vic Broughton

Sam Cooke

Sam Cooke, born in Clarksdale, was the son of a Baptist minister and sang with a family group, the Singing Children. The family moved to Chicago where the teenaged Cooke sang with the "Highway QC's" in the Highway Baptist Church. He later joined the legendary gospel quartet the Soul Stirrers, which he left to sing R&B. The gospel feeling was always a basis of his music, and he was known as the first gospel singer to bring in the younger crowd as well as the older fans.

RCA Victor signed Sam Cooke in 1960 after he'd already had several R&B hits for Specialty Records ("You Send Me" on the Keen label). For Victor he produced three singles, and all six sides soared to the top of the charts; 1962: "Bring It On Home to Me"/"Having a Party;" 1962: "Somebody Have Mercy"/"Nothing Can Change This Love;" 1965: "Shake"/"A Change is Gonna Come."

Jerry Butler

Following in the crooner tradition established by Sam Cooke, Jerry Butler, a native of Sunflower, also left gospel to produce hits on both R&B and pop charts. He composed "For Your Precious Love" as an exercise in a high school class; in 1958 with the Impressions he recorded it as a hit. In 1960, he worked with Curtis Mayfield to produce the million-seller "He Will Break Your Heart." The introduction was a four-bar phrase borrowed from a song by the gospel Staples Singers.

Jimmy Reed

Jerry Butler

Jimmy Reed

Bluesman Jimmy Reed from Leland had a steady boogie beat that appealed to dancing R&B fans. Reed was a regular occupant of R&B charts 1955-1961, with hits like "Big Boss Man" and "Bright Lights, Big City."

David Ruffin, left

Mary Wilson

Mary Wilson, born in Greenville, was one of the original Supremes, Motown's most popular singing group, producing such hits as "Baby Love," "Stop in the Name of Love," "Where Did Our Love Go," and "Come See About Me." Mary Wilson was inducted into the Rock and Roll Hall of Fame in 1988.

David Ruffin

Born in Meridian in 1941, David Ruffin (left, above) was the lead singer of the Temptations on such smash 1960s hits as "My Girl" and "I Wish it Would Rain."

Prentiss Barnes

Born in Magnolia, Barnes was the lead singer of the Moonglows, who during the 50s played packed clubs across the country, including New York's Apollo Theater and Carnegie Hall. Some of their best known hits were "Sincerely," "When I'm With You," and "Secret Love."

Prentiss Barnes, center, bottom

ACE ACE ACE ACE ACE ACE ACE

JIMMY CLANTON
FRANKIE FORD
HUEY "PIANO" SMITH
THE CLOWNS
AMOS MILBURN
IKE CLANTON
AL WARD
JOE TEX
EARL KING
HARRY LEE
BAT CARROLL
EARL WILLIAMS
CHARLES BROWN
BOBBY MARCHAN
JOHNNY FAIRCHILD
ALVIN "RED" TYLER

ACE RECORDS INC., JACKSON, MISSISSIPPI

Records and Recording

During the late 40s Jimmy Ammons opened Delta Records, a recording studio in Jackson. It was the first studio in the state to employ mixers—more than one microphone was mixed in—and performers included Cool Cat Cannon, the original Mississippi Rolling Stones (predating the English version), Little Milton Campbell, Tommy Lee, and a young Elvis Presley playing backup guitar.

Johnny Vincent (John Vincent Imbragulio) started recording in 1948 on the Champion label. His first artist was Big Boy Crudup, and he also recorded Guitar Slim for Specialty Records. Vincent started Ace, "his big one," in 1954 and had hits with Earl King, Jimmy Clanton, Frankie Ford, and Huey Smith. Other labels he produced were Pink, Vin, Spiral, and Rich, all of them R&B or pop.

"I like to produce music that makes people move. They might want to shake, they might want to dance, and they might want to fight. But they all want to move."

Johnny Vincent

Ace Records Founder

Earl King and Johnny Vincent

Malaco Records, founded in Jackson in 1968 by Tommy Couch and Mitchell Malouf, won its first Gold Record early with the R&B hit "Groove Me," by King Floyd, followed by more gold with Jean Knight's "Mr. Big Stuff" and Dorothy Moore's "Misty Blue." The Company soon branched out to include gospel and blues, recording hit albums by Z.Z. Hill, Little Milton Campbell, Bobby "Blue" Bland, Johnny Taylor, and many more.

Stax Records in Memphis produced Mississippi soul artists like the Bar-Kays, Rufus Thomas, and his daughter Carla Thomas. The Stax artists took "soul" – R&B with an urban twist – around the world.

ALLSTARS

Bar-Kays
Jewel Bass/*Jackson*
Pat Brown/*Jackson*
Jerry Butler/*Sunflower*
Ace Campbell/*Grenada*
"Little" Milton
Campbell/*Inverness*
Sam Cannon
"Little" Milton Cooke
Cozy Corley and the Blue
Gardenias/*Hattiesburg*
Tyrone Davis/*Greenville*
Jim Easterling/*Marion County*
Betty Everett/*Glenwood*
C. L. Franklin/*Clarksdale*
Lummy French
Bill Gayle/*Clarksdale*
John Lee Hooker/*Clarksdale*
Eddie Houston/*Meridian*
Thelma Houston/*Leland*
Luther "Guitar" Johnson/*Itta
Bena*
Eddie "Guitar Slim"
Jones/*Greenwood*
Sonny Landruth/*Canton*
Denise LaSalle/*Belzoni*
Glenn "Tany" Lott/*Grenada*
Dorothy Moore/*Jackson*
Patrice Moncell/*Jackson*
Clem Moorman
Junior Parker/*Clarksdale*
Jimmy Reed/*Leland*
Jesse Robinson/*Jackson*
David Ruffin,
Temptations/*Meridian*
Bobby Rush/*Jackson*
Otis Rush/*Philadelphia*
Oliver Sain/*Dundee*
Judson Spence/*Pascagoula*
The Tangents/*Cleveland*

Luther "Guitar Junior" Johnson

Tommy Tate/*Jackson*
Eddie "Playboy" Taylor/*Benoit*
"Little" Johnny Taylor
Rufus Thomas/*Cayce*
Ike Turner/*Clarksdale*
Jim Weatherly/*Pontotoc*
Carson Whitsett/*Jackson*
Mary Wilson,
Supremes/*Greenville*

Thelma Houston

Dorothy Moore

ROCK AND ROLL
BLUES HAD A BABY, CALLED IT ROCK AND ROLL

ROCK AND ROLL, LIKE THE BLUES, WAS BORN in the South and was the answer to the younger generation's need for a wide-open music, danceable and spirited, that R&B music was meeting for black audiences. In juke joints, blues singers noticed the change. James "Son" Thomas says, "When I played at a Saturday night dance, they always wanted to do the slow drag. Some calls it the snake hip. But now the young people are all on fast time. They swing out. The one you dance with is over there and you way over here."

79

Jackie Brenston

Rock and roll was slowly gaining a place in American popular music, but there was still much of the forties "pop" music of the kind featured on shows like "Hit Parade." Bored young people all over the South were tuning in to late-night black R&B stations like Randy's Record Mart in Galveston, Tennessee, and others; and by the 1950s "rock and roll," an old term that had been in increasingly heavy use since the 30s, was used to describe many kinds of "new" music, including the sensual rhythm and blues brand and

an emerging rockabilly brand.

One serious contender for the first rock and roll record is "Rocket '88," written by Mississippians James Cotton and Ike Turner and recorded by Clarksdale's Jackie Brenston (backed by Ike Turner's Delta Cats). Sam Phillips recorded it in his Memphis studios, then sold it to Chess Records in 1951, when it became a number one hit.

Ike Turner and the Rhythm Kings

Ike Turner

Ike Turner of Clarksdale, a musician himself, became a scout for the Modern record label. When asked if there was any more talent around the state like him, Ike replied, "Lots of it. All over Mississippi." Through Ike, Modern recorded Howlin' Wolf, Elmore James, B. B. King, and others. Later Ike left Mississippi with his band, the Kings of Rhythm, and went to St. Louis, where he met his future wife and partner, Tina.

"Ike [Turner] was playing piano with Howlin' Wolf during the time that Rocket '88 Oldsmobiles had just come out.... This guy passed us in this Rocket '88. He was flying and Ike tried to catch him. I said, 'Man, you can't catch that man, he's driving a Rocket '88,' and that's how the song got started. Jackie Brenston came out with the song first, but me and Ike really wrote it."

James Cotton

"Oh, I know Ike Turner, oh, yeah, I knowed Ike. See, Ike is a Clarksdale boy, this boy Jackie Brenston, what make 'Rocket '88,' he's a Clarksdale boy, and I knowed all of them."

B.B. King

> *"I wasn't what you'd call a blues artist. I was put in the R&B lineup because they didn't know what the hell to call me, man. Finally, Alan Freed started calling me 'rock and roll.'"*
>
> **Bo Diddley**

Bo Diddley

Other artists provided a link between R&B and rock and roll. Bo Diddley (Ellas McDaniel) of McComb recorded a song called "Bo Diddley" in 1955. It was the top R&B seller of the year, but it was to provide inspiration to every rock and roll band after him. The song that made him famous was based, he says, on a "play party tune" from his Mississippi youth.

Since rock and roll was a relatively new term, the almost weekly hits of Bo Diddley, Little Walter, and Muddy Waters landed on the R&B charts.

The "Bo Diddley beat," something akin to the old "Shave and a haircut, two bits" rhythm, has since become a part of almost every rocker's repertoire—either as a straight cover of Bo Diddley or adapted with different lyrics.

Warren Smith

Lucky Joe

Rock and roll was blooming in Jackson in the 1950s. The gospel Trumpet label had already branched out to record blues, and in 1954, Joe Almond and his Hillbilly Rockers recorded "Gonna Roll and Rock" and "Rock Me" for Trumpet. Lucky Joe Almond opened the Grand Ole Opry for years with his "Rock Me," one of the first rock and roll records.

Warren Smith, from Louise, was a country singer with a strong rockabilly strain, and he recorded "Rock and Roll Ruby" in 1956 for Sun. He produced another hit, "Ubangi Stomp," written by Iuka's Charles Underwood, a songwriter/producer prominent in the beginnings of Sun Records.

Elvis Presley

Rockabilly was firmly rooted in country music but drew heavily on black gospel and rhythm and blues. First recorded by Sam Phillips on Sun Records in Memphis, Phillips' two major performers were Mississippians Elvis Presley and Jerry Lee Lewis.

Elvis Presley, born in Tupelo in 1935, is the most important figure in the history of rock and roll music. Elvis's first musical influence was the gospel music he heard as a child in the First Assembly of God Church in Tupelo, a branch of the Pentecostal movement and well known for its gospel music. He attended Sunday school classes with Cecil Blackwood of the later Blackwood Brothers, a group he admired. Elvis also listened to blues and rhythm and blues on Memphis radio stations.

In July of 1954, Elvis made his first record for Sam Phillips' Sun label: "Blue Moon of Kentucky" and "That's All Right Mama," which hit number one on the country charts. His next eight Sun sides, released between August 1954 and August 1955 included country, R&B, rockabilly, and blues. A Memphis disc jockey declared, "He's the new rage—sings hillbilly in R&B time."

Widespread recognition came in 1956 with the success of his first RCA Victor release, "Heartbreak Hotel"; a series of network television appearances; and a movie, "Love Me Tender."

When Elvis went to New York City in 1956 for his first appearance on television, on the Tommy Dorsey Show, he spent many hours at the Apollo Theatre. His favorite act was fellow Mississippian Bo Diddley of McComb.

From 1956 until his death in 1977, Elvis Presley's music was the dominant influence in American popular music.

"Mr. Phillips said he'd coach me if I'd come over to the studio as often as I could. It must have been a year and a half before he gave me an actual session. At last he let me try a western song—and it sounded terrible. 'You want to make some blues?' he suggested to me over the phone, knowing I'd always been a sucker for that jive. He mentioned Big Boy Crudup and maybe others. I don't remember. All I know is, I hung up and ran fifteen blocks to Mr. Phillips' office before he'd gotten off the line—or so he tells me."
Elvis Presley

Elvis Presley with Junior Parker, left, and Bobby "Blue" Bland, right

"He sings Negro rhythms with a white voice, which borrows in mood and emphasis from the country style, modified by popular music. It's a blend of them all."

Sam Phillips, Sun Records

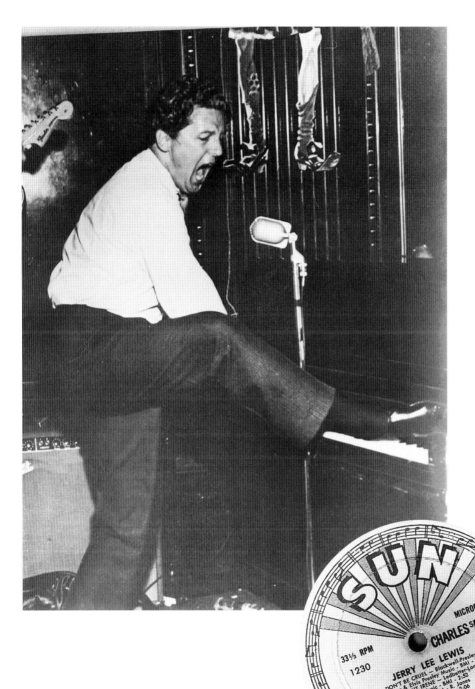

Jerry Lee Lewis

Born in Ferriday, Louisiana, across the Mississippi River from Natchez, Jerry Lee Lewis has performed or lived in Mississippi most of his life. Lewis played the piano at the Blue Cat Night Club in Natchez and had a regular program at WNAT in Natchez as a teenager. Inspired by Elvis's example, Lewis went to Memphis and persuaded Sam Phillips to record him. His first big hit, "Whole Lot of Shakin' Going On," was in the rockabilly tradition.

Rock & Roll's Debt to Mississippi Musicians

Today rock guitarists everywhere play with a metal or glass slider on their fingers, an homage to Delta bluesmen like Elmore James and Muddy Waters, who were also the first to explore the uses of feedback and distortion with electric guitars.

Keith Richards with Willie Dixon

Eric Clapton

"I'd never heard electric Delta blues before. It changed everything. It wasn't fancy or fast. It was just the deepest...I felt so much love for him [Muddy Waters]. I felt like he was my father, and I was his adopted son."

Eric Clapton, musician

"When I heard him [Muddy Waters] I realized the connection between all the music.... He was like the code book. I was incredibly inspired by him as a musician."

Keith Richards, Rolling Stones

"Robert Johnson was good, really good. If you want to take rock and roll he was the beginning of it... You can't hear a blues tune or a rock tune that don't have some of Robert's chords in it."

Johnny Shines, musician

"Went home, listened to Jimmie Rodgers on my lunch break." **From "Cleaning Windows," Van Morrison**

90

"Nothing really affected me until I heard Elvis. If there hadn't been an Elvis, there wouldn't have been the Beatles."
John Lennon, The Beatles

"He was an integrator. Elvis was a blessing. They wouldn't let black music through. He opened the door for black music."
Little Richard

"Elvis Presley made it possible for all of us to follow."
Buddy Holly

"This man [Elvis] was the number one thing in the world for twenty years."
Carl Perkins, musician

"For me he was the one standing on the highest mountain with the brightest light."
Robbie Robertson, musician

"When I first heard Elvis' voice I just knew that I wasn't going to work for anybody; and nobody was going to be my boss...Hearing him for the first time was like busting out of jail."
Bob Dylan, musician

ALLSTARS

Joe Almond and the Hillbilly
Rockers/*Jackson*
Blind Melon/*West Point*
Jackie Brenston/*Clarksdale*
Jimmy Buffet/*Pascagoula*
Ben Chester Carlisle
George Cartwright/*Belzoni*
Chambers Brothers/*Flora*
Joe Frank Corolla/*Leland*
Cracker Jacks/*Hattiesburg*
Paul Davis/*Meridian*
Dawnbreakers/*Jackson*
Drapes/*Hattiesburg*
Susan Elkins/*Hattiesburg*
Johnny Fairchild and the Night
Riders/*Hattiesburg*
Charlie Feathers/*Myrtle*
Bobby Field/*Hattiesburg*
Steve Forbert/*Meridian*
Gants
Arlan Gibson/*Meridian*
Cliff Granberry
Grass/*Starkville*
Graves Brothers/*Hattiesburg*
Nathanial "Nate Dogg" Hale
Eddie Houston/*Meridian*
Raymond Hill
Ray Hunter
Cordell Jackson/*Pontotoc*
Harold Lloyd "Conway Twitty"
Jenkins/*Friars Point*
Jesse Knight
Reggie Knighton/*Biloxi*
Freddy Knoblock/*Jackson*
Tim Lee/*Jackson*
Let's Eat/*Jackson*
Jerry Lee Lewis/*Ferriday/Natchez*
Little David and the Giants/*Laurel*

Ellas "Bo Diddley"
McDaniel/*McComb*
"Little" John Marascalo
Mac McAnally
Amos Morgan
My Generation/*Natchez*
Omar and the
Howlers/*Hattiesburg*
Oral Sox/*Jackson*
Elvis Presley/*Tupelo*
Jerry Puckett/*Jackson*
Frank Saxton
Red Tops/*Vicksburg*
Frazier Riddell/*Canton*
Rock Project/*Jackson*
Royal American Show
Band/*Jackson*

Rolling Stones/*Jackson*
Frank Saxton
Warren Smith/*Louise*
Substantial Evidence/*Biloxi*
Bobby Sutliff/*Jackson*
The Tangents/*Cleveland*
Greg "Fingers" Taylor/*Jackson*
T-Birds
Ike Turner/*Clarksdale*
The Twilites/*Hattiesburg*
Tim Whitsett and the
Imperials/*Jackson*
Webb Wilder and the
Beatnecks/*Hattiesburg*
Windbreakers/*Jackson*
Zero Pop

Andy Anderson and the Original Rolling Stones

Omar and the Howlers

Fred Knoblock

Webb Wilder

The Tangents

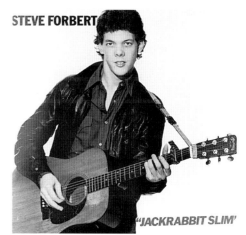

Steve Forbert

Jimmy Buffet

Tim Whitsett and the Imperial Show Band

The Twilites

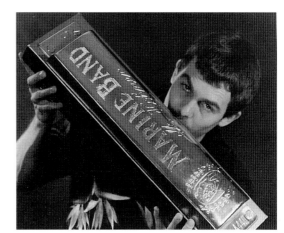

Fingers Taylor

JAZZ

LIKE THE BLUES, JAZZ IS AN AFRICAN-AMERICAN FORM. That is, it did not originate in Africa or Europe but in America, reflecting those two musical traditions but also many others. Jazz was made from the same elements as the blues, but with very different emphases. Improvisation, for example, was important to the blues; in jazz, improvisation was elevated so that it became the essence of the art.

As early as 1835, brass bands were formed on southern plantations, bands imitating pre-Revolutionary British

bands. From these grew minstrel bands, jug or jook bands, and the ragtime style—precursors of jazz.

"Blues is the same as jazz. Jazz grew out of the blues."

B.B. King, musician

> *"Listen to Coltrane or Miles Davis and you'll hear wordless blues that go back to field hollers and slavery times."*
> **Peter Guralnick, music historian**

> *"Man, they'd have a big time...They called them the Nigger Minstrels and the Ringling Brothers, they had a big show."*
> **Sam Chatmon, bluesman**

Minstrel Show

As minstrel shows set up, brass bands would parade around to drum up an audience. Shows played outside small towns, at levee camps, and at plantations.

"Blackface" minstrel music was performed by both black and white performers, who rubbed cork on their faces for the roles. Minstrelsy began in the 1820s and peaked 1850-1870, but the tradition remained strong well into the twentieth century. Minstrel shows featured all kinds of music—blues, Tin Pan Alley tunes, country, and ragtime. One of the most popular shows, the Rabbit Foot Minstrels, was organized by F. S. Wolcott of Port Gibson. The Rabbit Foot Show featured Ma Rainey, Sam Chatmon, Rufus Thomas, and a star drummer from Vicksburg, Joseph Thomas Dorsey, called the best drummer ever by Jellyroll Morton.

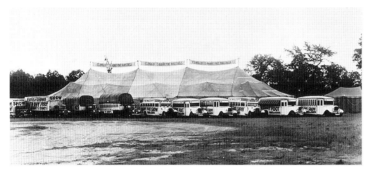

F.S. Wolcott Rabbit Foot Minstrels

"My father was a musi-cian—with F. S. Wolcott's Rabbit Foot Minstrels show—most of his life. What kind of music is that?"
Son Seals, bluesman

"It was a good show... comedians...oh, they'd cut up...Had all that cork on our faces...made us look even blacker...painted our mouths white."
Gus Cannon

Minstrel bands and street bands featured highly complex rhythmic syncopation, despite their humble instruments. Bands paraded around towns while roustabouts rigged tents. A popular form of minstrel music was the jug band or jook band, featuring homemade or primitive instruments.

Esau McGee of Greenville with his homemade bass.

"I think that the average jazz musician can play the blues better than the average blues musician because the jazz musician that came up through the church as a lot of them did, when they go into jazz it's like you come through elementary school, then high school, then on to college."

B.B. King, musician

"Jazz is syncopated blues. When I was young, spirituals like "Swing Low, Sweet Chariot" would be syncopated and turned into a jazz tune."

Willie Dixon, musician

Jim Jackson

By the 1920s, in larger cities especially in the North, the terms jazz and blues were almost synonymous. Jazz bands, black and white, played and recorded blues. Travelers on the Mississippi River heard bands playing ragtime and a music called Dixieland. In 1928, W. C. Handy, who had popularized the blues in a format closely akin to jazz, conducted a jazz show at Carnegie Hall. "Jazz" players were turning up all over: Louis Armstrong backed Jimmie Rodgers, the "Singing Brakeman," in the late 30s on "Blue Yodel No. 9" for Victor records, producing some fine jazz-tinged country music. The Mississippi Sheiks recorded "The Jazz Fiddler" in 1930. Jim Jackson of Hernando recorded one of the biggest hits of the 1920s – "Jim Jackson's Kansas City Blues Parts 1 & 2" – a minstrel blues number.

As the piano gained importance in blues and jazz, the trumpet held its lead in the brass jazz band. The instrument that slowly came to symbolize jazz, however, was growing in popularity: the saxophone.

Gus Cannon

Gus Cannon, born in Red Banks in 1883, was raised on a plantation, where he made a banjo from a frying pan and learned to play it. He joined a travelling medicine show organized by Dr. Stokey of Clarksdale and began a career in minstrel music, operating in tents and on the backs of trucks or wagons. In 1910 he met Noah Lewis of Ripley and soon Lewis was playing harp (harmonica) with Cannon's oilcan "jug" in a band called Gus Cannon's Jug Stompers.

"Lawd, he used to blow the hell outa that harp. He could play two harps at the same time, through his mouth and nose, same key, same melody. Y'know he could wrap his lips 'round the harp and his nose was just like a fist."

Gus Cannon on harp player
Noah Lewis

"Some people call it a garbage can, but I call it a streamline bass."

Will Shade, musician

Jug made and used by Gus Cannon. The jug was a cheap alternative to the double bass, giving out a low-pitched buzzing sound when blown at different angles.

The washboard was used as a percussion instrument, played with a thimble or the bare hand.

"Prez" Lester Young

Lester Young (1909-1959), born in Woodville, is considered one of jazz's most innovative improvisors. As a star of Count Basie's band and popular accompanist to singer Billie Holiday, Young introduced a new style of saxophone playing that became standard to later generations. The almost vocal inflections of his playing and his harmonic ideas influenced jazz heavily for the next twenty years. The 1987 movie "Round Midnight" was based largely on the life of Lester Young.

"Everybody of my generation listened to Lester Young and almost no one else. Lester's influence was all-embracing and touched Miles Davis, John Lewis, Lee Konitz, Gerry Mulligan, Stan Getz, and other adherents of the "cool" school that dominated jazz in the early 50s."

Dexter Gordon

Sweethearts of Rhythm

Piney Woods Country Life School near Braxton produced not only fine gospel groups but also internationally known jazz musicians. The "Swinging Rays of Rhythm," an all-girl, integrated swing jazz band, played around Jackson during the 1930s. Another similar group with some of the same musicians, called the "Sweethearts of Rhythm," broke off from Piney Woods and toured widely, eventually playing the Apollo Theatre in New York. At the peak of their career they toured Europe during World War II, entertaining troops.

102

Teddy Edwards

Jackson native Teddy Edwards, born in 1924, played jazz in the parking lots of drive-in restaurants as a teenager and at the Crystal Palace on Farish Street. After he travelled with the Doc Parmley band, Edwards moved to California, where he became famous for his style of playing the saxophone, emphasizing, as Young and Hinton had, the new styles of playing and favoring improvisation over the more set "swing" jazz. Edwards was a key figure in the formation of the new "bebop" school of jazz on the West Coast while Hinton had opened up jazz on the East.

"I learned everything I know about music from the book my daddy left sitting on the piano, a book about harmony."
Teddy Edwards

Milt Hinton, "The Judge"

Born in Vicksburg in 1910, Milt Hinton was exposed in his youth to "strollers," improvisational musicians who strolled the streets at night and played for nickels and dimes. When Hinton got to New York, he became bass player for the Cab Calloway orchestra, where he remained from 1936 through the early 1950s. Then Hinton began to shake the conventions of swing jazz and to experiment with a free new style that was later called bebop. Hinton, called "The Judge" because of his tenure in the business, became the role model for a generation of jazz musicians.

Mose Allison

Born in Tippo, pianist, singer, and songwriter Mose Allison grew up hearing piano blues in the Delta. He performed with Zoot Sims, Gerry Mulligan, and Stan Getz before going solo with his sophisticated, ironic songs that retain a strong blues inflection.

Freddie Waits

Born in Jackson in 1943, Freddie Waits played drums and flute with Sonny Rollins, McCoy Tyner, Freddie Hubbard, and Lena Horne, among others, and toured with Ella Fitzgerald 1967-68. He also achieved international fame through his work with the M'Boom percussion group. *Downbeat* magazine called him "a resourceful drummer with fire and taste."

"Mississippi was my roots and my foundation. Detroit was the body. New York was the brainy part, where I began to slick up."
Freddie Waits

Mose Allison

Freddie Waits

Gerald Wilson

A native of Shelby, Gerald Wilson, in addition to leading and recording his own band, performed with bands of Jimmy Lunceford, Count Basie, Duke Ellington, and Dizzy Gillespie.

Delta Rythm Boys

Lee Gaines of Buena Vista founded the Delta Rhythm Boys, a jazz and vocal pop group that was internationally acclaimed for over fifty years, best known during the 1940s and 1950s. The quartet recorded with Count Basie and Ella Fitzgerald and were the first black entertainers to play Las Vegas. The appeared in over 35 feature and musical films.

ALLSTARS

McRae Adams/*Jackson*
Charlie Allen/*Jackson*
Mose Allison/*Tippo*
Jules Barlow
Walter Barnes/*Vicksburg*
Harry King Barth/*Natchez*
George Bean
Frederic Beckett/*Nettleton*
James Bertrand
Andrew Blakney/*Quitman*
Walter Bonds/*Natchez*
Bobby Bradford/*Cleveland*
London Branch/*Jackson*
Army Brown/*Jackson*
Donald Brown/*DeSoto County*
Melvin Brown
Richard Brown/*Jackson*
Michael Neely Bryan/*Byhalia*
Bobby Bryant/*Hattiesburg*
Ed Butler
Gus Cannon/*Red Banks*
George Cartwright/*Belzoni*
Jimmy Claybrooke
Curlew
Olu Dara/*Natchez*
Charles Davis/*Goodman*

Coot Davis
Delta Rhythm Boys
Joseph Thomas Dorsey/*Vicksburg*
James Dudley/*Hattiesburg*
Joe Dyson /*Jackson*
Jim Easterling
Theodore "Teddy"
Edwards/*Jackson*
Black Emile/*Hattiesburg*
Alvin Fielder/*Meridian*
William Fielder/*Meridian*
William Fischer/*Shelby*
Herman Fowlkes/*Jackson*
Andrew Fox
Lee Gaines/*Buena Vista*
Burgess Gardener
John Gilmore/*Summit*
Bruce Golden/*Jackson*
Dick Griffin/*Jackson*
John "Captain"
Handy/*Pass Christian*
Mark Hannah
Andy Hardwick/*Jackson*
"Dump" Harvey/*Jackson*
Erskine Hawkins
James Hemphill/*Summit*
Arthur "Art" Hillary/*Jackson*
Milton "The Judge"

Hinton/*Vicksburg*
Herbie Holmes/*Yazoo City*
Miller Holmes/*Yazoo City*
Robert Holmes/*Greenville*
Isaac "Red" Holt
Blind Homer/*Hattiesburg*
Mark Howell/*Philadelphia*
Duke Huddleston/*Jackson*
Shep Hunter/*Crystal Springs*
Jim Jarrett
Joe Jennings/*Natchez*
Lawrence Johnson
Oliver "Dink" Johnson/*Biloxi*
Hank Jones/*Vicksburg*
Jug Stompers
Tim Kelly
Louis Lee/*Hazlehurst*
Robert E. Lee
Mundell Lowe/*Laurel*
Charles Magee/*Laurel*
John McCauley
Tim McGivern/*Natchez*
Skeets McWilliams
The Mississippians
Mississippi Jook Band
Mulgrew Miller/*Greenwood*
Monkey Joe/*Hattiesburg*
Brew Moore

Red Tops

Cassandra Wilson

Alvin Fielder

Edward "Moon" Mullen/*Mayhew*
Doc Parmley
Luke Parmley
Annie Pavageaux/*Columbus*
Gus Perryman/*Hattiesburg*
B.J. Prescott/*Hattiesburg*
Eugene "Gene" Porter/*Jackson*
Dick Prenshaw
Edwin McIntosh Quinn/*McComb*
Henry Reed
Butch Roseby
Britt Roseby
Jimmy Rowan/*Natchez*
Dewey Sampson/*Jackson*
I. S. Sanders, Jr./*Jackson*
Raphael Semmes
Bud Scott/*Natchez*
Jack Scott
Emmet Slater
Dalton Smith/*Forest*
Leo Smith /*Leland*
Otis Smith and the Footwarmers/*Natchez*
Larel Sonelous Smith /*Hillhouse*
Mike Strickland/*Jackson*
Lucius Stokes

Napoleon Strickland/*Como*
Sweethearts of Rhythm/*Piney Woods*
Huey Swift
Swinging Rays of Rhythm/*Piney Woods*
Toby Tenhet/*Drew*
Benjamin "Ben" Thigpen/*Laurel*
Tophatters
Boland Townsend
Cooney Vaughn/*Hattiesburg*
Charles Underwood/*Iuka*
Frederick "Freddy" Waits/*Jackson*
Blake Wadsworth/*Natchez*
Leon "Diamond" Washington/*Jackson*
Joseph Watts/*Jackson*
Lloyd Wells/*Ellisville*
Joe White/*Vicksburg*
Charlie Wicker/*Jackson*
Reginald Willis/*Jackson*
Cassandra Wilson/*Jackson*
Stanley Gerald Wilson/*Shelby*
Lester "Prez" Young/*Woodville*
Zero Pop/*Jackson*

Othar Turner's Fife and Drum

Photograph/Illustration Credits

cover, Elvis Presley and B. B. King (Ernest Withers, Center for Southern Folklore)

p. 1, dobro (David Evans, Delta Blues Museum)

p. 2, Dockery Farms (Tom Rankin)

p. 3, "High Water Everywhere" (Stefan Grossman, *Delta Blues Guitar)*

p. 4, blues club (Marion Post Wolcott, Library of Congress)

p. 5, rural Mississippi scene (Frederick Ramsey)

p. 6, guitar ad, Sears, Roebuck catalog, 1897; Sam Chatmon (Patti Black)

p. 7, harmonica (Delta Blues Museum); *Blues: An Anthology* (Delta Blues Museum); W. C. Handy (Blues Archive, University of Mississippi)

p. 8, WROX microphone (Delta Blues Museum); Sonny Boy Williamson and King Biscuit Time (Delta Blues Museum)

p. 9, "22-20 Blues" record label (Gayle Dean Wardlow);"Spoonful Blues" and "Pea Vine Blues" posters (Stefan Grossman, *Delta Blues Guitar)*

p. 10, "Catfish Blues" record label and photos Willie Love and Sonny Boy Williamson (Lillian McMurry, Blues Archive, University of Mississippi); Elmore James (Blues Archive, University of Mississippi)

p. 11, Charley Patton (Blues Archive, University of Mississippi); "Down the Dirt Road Blues" and "High Water Everywhere" (Stefan Grossman, *Delta Blues Guitar)*

p. 12, Robert Johnson dimestore photo (Stephen C. LaVere); Robert Johnson album cover (Columbia Records); Robert Johnson monument (Christine Wilson)

p. 13, Tommy Johnson (Blues Archive, University of Mississippi); Son House (Dick Waterman)

p. 14, Mississippi John Hurt and Skip James (Dick Waterman); Bukka White (Arhoolie Records)

p. 15, Jack Owens (Eyd Kazery); Houston Stackhouse, Sonny Boy Williamson, Peck Curtis (Chris Strachwitz)

p. 16, Charlie Musselwhite (Charlie Musselwhite); Cleveland "Broom-Man" Jones (Eyd Kazery)

p. 17, Son Thomas (David Rae Morris)

p. 18, Fred McDowell, Arthur "Big Boy" Crudup, and Robert Pete Williams (Dick Waterman)

p. 19, John Anderson Brown (WPA Folk Music Tour collection, Mississippi Department of Archives and History)

p. 20, shape note singing (WPA Folk Music Tour collection, Mississippi Department of Archives and History)

p. 21, Blackwood Brothers (James Blackwood); Blackwood Brothers record label and "My Heart's in Mississippi" record label (Sam Wilkins)

p. 22, Claunch Family, (Carl Fleischhauer)

p. 23, Chatmon Family (Ray Funk); Mississippi Sheiks (Blues Archive, University of Mississippi)

p. 24, violin advertisement (Sears, Roebuck catalog, 1897); John Hatcher (WPA Folk Music Tour collection, Mississippi Department of Archives and History)

p. 25, Ernest Claunch, children on porch, and Kitrells (WPA Folk Music tour collection, Mississippi Department of Archives and History)

p. 26, Hoyt Ming and the Pep Steppers (Carl Fleischhauer); Slim Scoggins and the Roamin' Cowboys (Mississippi Department of Archives and History)

p. 27, Leake County Revelers (Carl Fleischhauer)

p. 28, unidentified string band, and radio broadcast (WPA Folk Music Tour collection, Mississippi Department of Archives and History)

p. 29, Jimmie Rodgers (Jimmie Rodgers Museum)

p. 30, Jimmie Rodgers railroad jacket, cap, lantern and songbook (Country Music Foundation)

p. 31, Charley Pride (Country Music Foundation); Frank Floyd (Eyd Kazery)

p. 32, O. B. McClinton, Tammy Wynette, Conway Twitty (Country Music Foundation)

p. 33, Blackwood Brothers, later generation (Country Music Foundation)

p. 34, Faith Hill (Warner Bros.); Canoy Wildcats (Mississippi Department of Archives and History)

p. 35, Marty Stuart (MCA Records); Jim Weatherly (Jim Weatherly)

p. 36, Jimmy Swan (Blues Archive, University of Mississippi); Bobbie Gentry (Capitol); and Paul Overstreet (RCA)

p. 37, Fisk Jubilee Singers (Fisk University)

p. 38, Utica Jubilee Quartet (Ben Bailey)

p. 39, Rural church (WPA Folk Music Tour Collection, Mississippi Department of Archives and History)

p. 40, rural church exterior and church service (Mississippi Department of Archives and History)

p. 41, Cotton Blossom Singers and "Commencement Day at Piney Woods" (Piney Woods Country Life School)

p. 42, Five Blind Boys publicity shot (Ethel Brown Williams); on stage (Ray Funk)

p. 43, Staples Singers record album (Stax); "Pop" Staples (Christine Wilson); on stage (Mississippi Valley Collection, Memphis State University)

p. 44, Charles Price Jones (Richard Beadle Collection, Mississippi Department of Archives and History); C. H. Mason (Ray Funk)

p. 45, C. L. Franklin (Jeff Titon, courtesy Erma Franklin)

p. 46, Soul Stirrers record album (Rebecca Pittman); Soul Stirrers (Ray Funk)

p. 47, Willard and Lillian McMurry (Lillian McMurry); Southern Sons (Ray Funk); "Oh, Lord I'm in Your Care" record label (Lillian McMurry)

p. 48, choir (Center for Southern Folklore)

p. 49, Cleophus Robinson (Ray Funk); Frank Williams (Malaco Records)

p. 50, Utica Quartet (Mississippi Department of Archives and History); The Christianaires (Malaco Records)

p. 51, The Seven Stars (Mississippi Department of Archives and History); Willie Banks and the Messengers (Malaco Records); Eddie and the Corinthians (Mississippi Department of Archives and History); Jackson Southernairs (Malaco)

p. 52, Williams Brothers, Mississippi Mass Choir (Malaco Records); Canton Spirituals (Mississippi Department of Archives and History)

p. 53, electric guitar (Jay Barkley) and amp (Geoffrey Wilson); harmonica (Fingers Taylor)

p. 54, Big Joe Williams (Eyd Kazery)

p. 55, Big Bill Broonzy (Yannick Bruynoghe, Chicago Historical Society)

p. 56, Howlin' Wolf at Silvio's, Chicago (Ray Flerlage, courtesy Robert Koester, Chicago Historical Society)

p. 57, Sonny Boy Williamson (Blues Archive, University of Mississippi); Charlie Musselwhite (Falk & Morrow Talent); Big Walter Horton (Arhoolie Records); James Cotton (Alligator Records)

p. 58, "Sad Letter Blues" record label (Delta Blues Museum); Muddy Waters (Eyd Kazery)

p. 59, Howlin' Wolf (Showtime Music Productions,Inc.)

p. 60, Willie Dixon (Willie Dixon)

p. 61, B. B. King (Dick Waterman)

p. 62, Otis Rush (Evidence Records); Otis Spann (Blues Archive, University of Mississippi)

p. 63, Albert King (STAX Records); Hartley Peavey (Peavey Electronics)

p. 64, Japanese poster and photo, Willie Dixon at Orly Airport (Robert Koester, Chicago Historical Society)

p. 65, Russian poster, Italian poster, Mexican poster (Blues Archive, University of Mississippi)

p. 66, Big Jack Johnson (Christine Wilson); Pinetop Perkins (Eyd Kazery); Eddie Clearwater (Blues Archive, University of Mississippi); Honeyboy Edwards (John G. Rockwood); Big Daddy Hood (Christine Wilson)

p. 67, Temptations (Motown)

p. 68, Jackson club (Richard Beadle photograph collection, Mississippi Department of Archives and History); Black Swan, Vocalion Race Records sleeves, Peacock and Bluebird labels (Blues Archive, University of Mississippi)

p. 69, Big Boy Crudup (Dick Waterman); "She's Gone" label (Delta Blues Museum)

p. 70, Rufus Thomas and Rufus Thomas onstage (Robert Barclay); "Bear Cat" poster (Blues Archive, University of Mississippi)

p. 71, Guitar Slim (Institute of Jazz Studies, Rutgers University); Junior Parker (Blues Archive, University of Mississippi); "The Things That I Used to Do" record (Blues Archive, University of Mississippi)

p. 72, John Lee Hooker (Eyd Kazery); album cover and "Hobo Blues" record label (Blues Archive, University of Mississippi)

p. 73, Sam Cooke (Ray Funk); "You Send Me" record label (Blues Archive, University of Mississippi); album covers (Rebecca Pittman)

p. 74, Jerry Butler (Rhino Records); poster (Blues Archive, University of Mississippi); Jimmy Reed (John G. Rockwood, Blues Archive, University of Mississippi)

p. 75, Mary Wilson (Mary Wilson); The Temptations (Motown); The Moonglows (Chess)

p. 76, Johnny Vincent and Earl King (Johnny Vincent); Ace Record and record sleeve (Ace Records)

p. 77, Bobby Bland, Denise LaSalle albums, and "Talking 'Bout Love"(Malaco Records)

p. 78, Luther "Guitar Junior" Johnson (Malaco); Thelma Houston (RCA Records); Dorothy Moore (Malaco Records)

p. 79, Elvis Presley poster (Hatch Show Print)

p. 80, Jackie Brenston (Jim O'Neal, Blues Archive, University of Mississippi); "Rocket '88" record (Delta Blues Museum)

p. 81, Ike Turner and the Kings of Rhythm (Blues Archive, University of Mississippi)

p. 82, Bo Diddley (Eyd Kazery); Bo Diddley and car (Blues Archive, University of Mississippi)

p. 83, Warren Smith (Colin Escott); Warren Smith record (Bobby Sutliff); Lucky Joe Almond and "Gonna Roll and Rock" record (Lillian McMurry, Blues Archive, University of Mississippi)

p. 84, Elvis Presley Show poster (Hatch Show Print)

p. 85, Elvis Presley (Graceland)

p. 86, Elvis Presley photo, shoes, gold record (Graceland)

p. 87, Elvis Presley with Bobby Blue Bland and Junior Parker (Ernest C. Withers courtesy Stephen C. LaVere)

p. 88, Elvis Presley RCA singles and Sun Collection (Margaret White)

p. 89, Jerry Lee Lewis photo (Colin Escott), Sun label record, album cover, shirt (Country Music Foundation)

p. 90, Eric Clapton (publicity still); Willie Dixon and Keith Richards (Blues Archive, University of Mississippi)

p. 91, Buddy Holly (publicity still); Little Richard (publicity still); John Lennon (publicity still)

p. 92, Andy Anderson and the Original Rolling Stones (Andy Anderson)

p. 93, Fred Knoblock (Fred Knoblock); Webb Wilder (Webb Wilder); The Tangents (Steve Morrison); Steve Forbert (CBS); Omar and the Howlers (Kent Dykes)

p. 94, Jimmy Buffett (Blues Archive, University of Mississippi); Tim Whitsett and the Imperial Show Band (Tim Whitsett); Fingers Taylor (Fingers Taylor); The Twilites (The Twilites)

p. 95, brass band (Frederick Ramsey)

p. 96, minstrel show (Library of Congress); Rabbit Foot poster photo (Frederick Ramsey)

p. 97, F. S. Wolcott Rabbit Foot Minstrels (Mississippi Department of Archives and History)

p. 98, rural scene and home-made bass (Frederick Ramsey)

p. 99, Jim Jackson (Blues Archive, University of Mississippi)

p. 100, Memphis Jug Band poster (Victor Records); Gus Cannon photo (Blues Archive, University of Mississippi); jug, washboard (David Tillman); homemade bass (Bill Ferris)

p. 101, Lester Young (Institute of Jazz Studies, Rutgers University)

p. 102, Sweethearts of Rhythm (Piney Woods Country Life School)

p. 103, Teddy Edwards (Institute of Jazz Studies, Rutgers University)

p. 104, Milt Hinton (Institute of Jazz Studies, Rutgers University)

p. 105, Mose Allison (Mose Allison); Freddie Waits (Christine Wilson)

p. 106, Delta Rhythm Boys (Institute of Jazz Studies, Rutgers University); Gerald Wilson (United Artists)

p. 107, Red Tops (Blues Archive, University of Mississippi)

p. 108, Cassandra Wilson (Eyd Kazery); Othar Turner's Fife and Drum (Blues Archive, University of Mississippi); Alvin Fielder (Alvin Fielder)

The Mississippi Department of Archives and History attempted to contact all photograph copyright owners regarding publication of these photographs. Individuals or institutions who did not receive a notice are invited to notify the Department for appropriate compensation.

Bibliography

Bailey, Ben E. *Music in the Life of a Free Black in Natchez.* Typescript, 1985.

Bane, Michael. *White Boy Singin' the Blues: Black Roots of White Rock.* New York: Penguin, 1982.

Bastin, Bruce. *Red River Blues: The Blues Tradition in the Southeast.* Urbana: University of Illinois Press, 1986.

Berry, Jason, and Jonathan Foose. *Up From the Cradle of Jazz: New Orleans Music Since World War II.* Athens: University of Georgia Press, 1986.

Charters, Samuel. *The Bluesmen: The Story and the Music of the Men Who Made the Blues.* New York: Oak Publications, 1967.

Charters, Samuel. *The Country Blues.* New York: Rinehart, 1959.

Clarke, Donald. *Penguin Encyclopedia of Pop Music.* London, 1989.

Cobb, Buell E. *The Sacred Harp: A Tradition and Its Music.* Athens: University of Georgia, 1978.

Cook, Bruce. *Listen to the Blues.* New York: Scribner's Sons, 1973.

Dixon, Robert, and John Godrich. *Recording the Blues.* New York: Stein and Day, 1970.

Dyson, Joe. Interview by Christine Wilson, 1988.

Escott, Colin, with Martin Hawkins. *Catalyst: The Sun Record Story.* London: Aquarius Books, 1975.

Epstein, Dena. *Sinful Tunes and Spirituals: Black Folk Music to the Civil War.* Urbana: University of Illinois Press, 1977.

Evans, David. *Big Road Blues: Tradition and Creativity in Folk Blues.* Berkeley: University of California Press, 1982.

Fahey, John. *Charley Patton.* London: Studio Vista, 1970.

Feather, Leonard. *The Encyclopedia of Jazz.* New York: Horizon Press, 1966.

Feather, Leonard. *The Encyclopedia of Jazz in the 70's.* New York: Horizon Press, 1976.

Fielder, Alvin. Interview by Christine Wilson, 1986.

Ferris, William. *Blues From the Delta: An Illustrated Documentary on Music and Musicians of the Mississippi Delta.* New York: Doubleday, 1979.

Ferris, William. *Mississippi Folk Voices.* Somerville, Mass.: Rounder Records, 1973.

Marcus, Greil. *Mystery Train: Images of American Rock 'n Roll Music.* New York: E. P. Dutton & Company, 1975.

Grossman, Stefan. *Delta Blues Guitar.* New York: Oak Publications, 1969.

Guralnick, Peter. *Listener's Guide to the Blues.* New York: Facts on File, 1982.

Guralnick, Peter. *Feel Like Going Home. Portraits in Blues and Rock and Roll.* New York: Vintage Books, 1981.

Guralnick, Peter. *Sweet Soul Music: Rhythm and Blues and the Dream of Freedom.* New York: Harper & Row, 1986.

Haralambos, Michael. *Right On: Blues to Soul.* New York: Drake Publishers, 1975.

Harris, Sheldon. *Blues Who's Who: A Biographical Dictionary of Blues Singers.* New Rochelle, N.Y.: Arlington House, 1979.

Johnson, James Weldon. *The Book of American Negro Spirituals.* New York: Viking, 1925.

Jones, LeRoi. *Blues People: Negro Music in White America.* New York: W. Morrow, 1963.

Keil, Charles. *Urban Blues.* Chicago: University of Chicago, 1966.

Leadbitter, Mike. *Nothing But the Blues.* London: Hanover, 1971.

Leadbitter, Mike. *Delta Country Blues.* Oxford: Thompson Harrison, Ltd., 1968.

Lomax, Alan. *Folk Songs of North America.* Garden City, N. Y.: Doubleday, 1960.

Lomax, John A. *Folk Song, U. S. A.* New York, 1947.

Lovell, John, Jr. *Black Song: The Forge and the Flame.* New York: Macmillan, 1972.

Mitchell, George. *Blow My Blues Away.* Baton Rouge: Louisiana State University Press, 1971.

Malone, Bill. *Country Music USA: A Fifty-Year History.* Austin: University of Texas Press, 1968.

Malone, Bill. *Southern Music/ American Music.* Lexington, University Press of Kentucky, 1979.

McKee, Margaret. *Beale Black and Blue: Life and Music on Black America's Main Street.* Baton Rouge: Louisiana State University Press, 1981.

McKinney, William A. *The Solid Rock.* Shannon, Miss.: McKinney Music Co., 1949.

Napier, Simon. *Back Woods Blues.* Bexhill-on-Sea, England: Blues Unlimited, 1968.

Neff, Robert, and Anthony Connor. *Blues.* Boston: Godine, 1975.

Oakley, Giles. *The Devil's Music: A History of the Blues.* New York: Harcourt, Brace, and Jovanovich, 1978.

Oliver, Paul. *The Meaning of the Blues.* New York: Collier Books, 1963.

Oliver, Paul. *The Story of the Blues.* Philadephia: Chilton, 1969.

Oliver, Paul, Max Harrison, and William Bolcom, editors. *New Grove Gospel, Blues and Jazz.* New York: W. W. Norton & Company, 1986.

Olsson, Bengt. *Memphis Blues and Jug Bands.* London: Studio Vista, 1970.

O'Neal, Jim. "Jackie Brenston," *Living Blues,* Tenth Anniversary Issue No. 45-46, 1980.

O'Neal, Jim. *"Living Blues* Interview: Lillian McMurry." *Living Blues,* No. 91, 1990.

Oster, Harry. *Living Country Blues.* New York: Minerva Press, 1975.

Palmer, Robert. *Deep Blues: A Musical and Cultural History of the Mississippi Delta.* New York: Penguin Books, 1982.

Pareles, Jon, and Patricia Romanowski. *The Rolling Stone Encyclopedia of Rock & Roll.* New York: Rolling Stone Press, 1983.

Pearson, Barry Lee. *Sounds So Good to Me: The Bluesman's Story.* Philadelphia: University of Pennsylvania, 1984.

Ramsey, Frederic, Jr. *Where the Music Started: A Photographic Essay*, New Brunswick, N J.: Rutgers University Press, 1970.

Ramsey, Frederic, Jr. *Been Here and Gone*. New Brunswick, N. J.: Rutgers University Press, 1960.

Sales, Grover. *Jazz: America's Classical Music*. Englewood Cliffs, N.J.: Prentice Hall, 1984.

Shaw, Arnold. *Black Popular Music in America: From the Spirituals, Minstrels, and Ragtime to Soul, Disco, and Hip Hop*. New York: Schermer, 1986.

Shaw, Arnold. *Honkers and Shouters: The Golden Years of Rhythm and Blues*. New York: McMillan, 1978.

Shaw, Arnold. *The World of Soul: Black America's Contribution to the Pop Music Scene*. New York: Collier, 1978.

Southern, Eileen. *The Music of Black Americans: A History*. New York: W. W. Norton, 1971.

Stambler, Irwin. *Encyclopedia of Pop, Rock, and Soul, Revised Edition*. New York: St. Martin's Press, 1989.

Stolper, Daryl. "Trumpet Records History." *Blues Unlimited,* No. 88, 1972.

Titon, Jeff Todd. *Early Downhome Blues.* Urbana: University of Illinois Press, 1977.

Titon, Jeff Todd. "Reverend C. L. Franklin: Black American Preacher-Poet" in Jabbour, Alan, and James Hardin, editors, *Folklife Annual,* 1987. Washington, D.C.: American Folklife Center at the Library of Congress, 1988.

Tosches, Nick. *Unsung Heroes of Rock and Roll.* New York: Scribner's Sons, 1984.

Ventura, Michael, "Hear That Long Snake Moan," *Whole Earth Review,* Spring and Summer, 1987.

Waits, Freddie. Interview by Christine Wilson, 1987.

Work, John. *American Negro Songs and Spirituals.* New York: Bonanza Books, 1940.

Index